D0324059

SCIENTIFIC AMERICAN™
CUTTING-EDGE SCIENCE™

Endangered Earth

ROSEN
PUBLISHING

New York

Published in 2008 by The Rosen Publishing Group, Inc.
29 East 21st Street, New York, NY 10010

Copyright © 2008 by Scientific American, Inc. All rights reserved.

No part of this book may be reproduced in any form without permission in writing from the publisher, except by a reviewer.

The articles in this book first appeared in the pages of *Scientific American*, as follows: "On the Termination of Species" by W. Wayt Gibbs, November 2001; "Cloning Noah's Ark" by Robert P. Lanza, Betsy L. Dresser and Philip Damiani, November 2000; "Rethinking Green Consumerism" by Jared Hardner and Richard Rice, May 2002; "The Unmet Need for Family Planning" by Malcolm Potts, January 2000; "Is Global Warming Harmful to Health?" by Paul R. Epstein, August 2000; "On Thin Ice?" by Robert A. Bindschadler and Charles R. Bentley, December 2002; "Meltdown in the North" by Matthew Sturm, Donald K. Perovich, and Mark C. Serreze, October 2003.

First Edition

Library of Congress Cataloging-in-Publication Data

Endangered Earth.
    p. cm.—(Scientific American cutting-edge science)
Includes index.
ISBN 13: 978-1-4042-1403-3 (library binding)
1. Environmental responsibility. I. Scientific American, Inc.
GE195.7.E54 2008
363.7—dc22

2007028638

Manufactured in Singapore

Illustration Credits: Cover The Earth (foreground): Nasa Goddard Space Flight Center Image by Reto Stockil (land surface, shallow water clouds). Enhancements by Robert Simmon(ocean color, compositing, 3-D globes, animation), Background images © Yong Hian Lim, i-stock, p. 12 Sarah Chen; p. 31 Laurie Grace; pp. 79, 88 Bryan Christie; p. 96 David Fierstein (main Antartic map), Robert A. Binschadler (ice thickness map), William F. Haxby (Florida map); pp. 98, 103 David Fierstein; p. 123 Lucy Reading.

On the cover: This true-color image of the Earth comes from NASA (National Aeronautics and Space Administration). Scientists combined a collection of satellite-based observations to create a seamless composite of the planet.

Table of Contents

Introduction

The climate is warming, species are disappearing and the human population continues to expand. Rarely does a day pass without these and other observations about the state of the planet making headlines. But what does it all really mean? And what, if anything, can be done about it?

In this book, leading experts discuss threats to life on Earth as we know it. Learn how rising temperatures are transforming polar landscapes and global epidemiology, how the current extinction rate compares with past ones and how inadequate access to contraceptives could severely impact the environment and health in coming years. Other articles explain how science might help preserve Earth's dwindling biodiversity, perhaps by cloning endangered species or marketing conservation services, for example.

Consider this a snapshot of our imperiled planet—with prescriptions for positive change.

—*The Editors*

I. "On the Termination of Species"

By W. Wayt Gibbs

Ecologists' warnings of an ongoing mass extinction are being challenged by skeptics and largely ignored by politicians. In part that is because it is surprisingly hard to know the dimensions of the die-off, why it matters and how it can best be stopped.

Hilo, Hawii—Among the scientists gathered here in August at the annual meeting of the Society for Conservation Biology, the despair was almost palpable. "I'm just glad I'm retiring soon and won't be around to see everything disappear," said P. Dee Boersma, former president of the society, during the opening night's dinner. Other veteran field biologists around the table murmured in sullen agreement.

At the next morning's keynote address, Robert M. May, a University of Oxford zoologist who presides over the Royal Society and until last year served as chief scientific adviser to the British government, did his best to disabuse any remaining optimists of their rosy outlook. According to his latest rough estimate, the extinction rate—the pace at which species vanish—accelerated during the past 100 years to roughly 1,000 times what it was before humans showed up. Various lines of argument, he explained, "suggest a speeding up by a further factor of 10 over the next century or so . . . . And that puts us squarely on the breaking edge of the sixth great wave of extinction in the history of life on Earth."

From there, May's lecture grew more depressing. Biologists and conservationists alike, he complained, are afflicted with a "total vertebrate chauvinism." Their bias toward mammals, birds and fish—when most of the diversity of life lies elsewhere—undermines scientists' ability to predict reliably the scope and consequences of biodiversity loss. It also raises troubling questions about the high-priority "hotspots" that environmental groups are scrambling to identify and preserve.

"Ultimately we have to ask ourselves why we care" about the planet's portfolio of species and its diminishment, May said. "This central question is a political and social question of values, one in which the voice of conservation scientists has no particular standing." Unfortunately, he concluded, of "the three kinds of argument we use to try to persuade politicians that all this is important . . . none is totally compelling."

Overview/Extinction Rates

- Eminent ecologists warn that humans are causing a mass extinction event of a severity not seen since the age of dinosaurs came to an end 65 million years ago. But paleontologists and statisticians have called such comparisons into doubt.
- It is hard to know how fast species are disappearing. Models based on the speed of tropical deforestation or on the growth of endangered species lists predict rising extinction rates. But biologists' bias toward plants and vertebrates, which represent a minority of life, undermine these predictions. Because 90 percent of species do not yet have names, let alone censuses, they are impossible to verify.
- In the face of uncertainty about the decline of biodiversity and its economic value, scientists are debating whether rare species should be the focus of conservation. Perhaps, some suggest, we should first try to save relatively pristine—and inexpensive—land where evolution can progress unaffected by human activity.

Although May paints a truly dreadful picture, his is a common view for a field in which best-sellers carry titles such as *Requiem for Nature*. But is despair justified? *The Skeptical Environmentalist*, the new English translation of a recent book by Danish statistician Bjørn Lomborg, charges that reports of the death of biodiversity have been greatly exaggerated. In the face of such external skepticism, internal uncertainty and public apathy, some scientists are questioning the conservation movement's overriding emphasis on preserving rare species and the threatened hotspots in which they are concentrated. Perhaps, they suggest, we should focus instead on saving something equally at risk but even more valuable: evolution itself.

Doom . . .

May's claim that humans appear to be causing a cataclysm of extinctions more severe than any since the one that erased the dinosaurs 65 million years ago may shock those who haven't followed the biodiversity issue. But it prompted no gasps from the conservation biologists. They have heard variations of this dire forecast since at least 1979, when Norman Myers guessed in *The Sinking Ark* that 40,000 species lose their last member each year and that one million would be extinct by 2000. In the 1980s Thomas Lovejoy similarly predicted that 15 to 20 percent would die off by 2000; Paul Ehrlich figured half would be gone by now. "I'm reasonably certain that [the elimination of one fifth of species] didn't happen," says Kirk O. Winemiller, a fish biologist at Texas A&M University who just finished a review of the scientific literature on extinction rates.

More recent projections factor in a slightly slower demise because some doomed species have hung on longer than anticipated. Indeed, a few have even returned from the grave. "It was discovered only this summer that the Bavarian vole, continental Eurasia's one and only presumed extinct mammal [since 1500], is in fact still with us," says Ross D. E. MacPhee, curator of mammalogy at the American Museum of Natural History (AMNH) in New York City.

Still, in the 1999 edition of his often-quoted book *The Diversity of Life*, Harvard University biologist E. O. Wilson cites current estimates that between 1 and 10 percent of species are extinguished every decade, at least 27,000 a year. Michael J. Novacek, AMNH's provost of science, wrote in a review article this spring that "figures approaching 30 percent extermination of all species by the mid-21st century are not unrealistic." And in a 1998 survey of biologists, 70 percent said they believed that a mass extinction is in progress; a third of them expected to lose 20 to 50 percent of the world's species within 30 years.

"Although these assertions of massive extinctions of species have been repeated everywhere you look, they do not equate with the available evidence," Lomborg argues in *The Skeptical Environmentalist*. A professor of statistics and political science at the

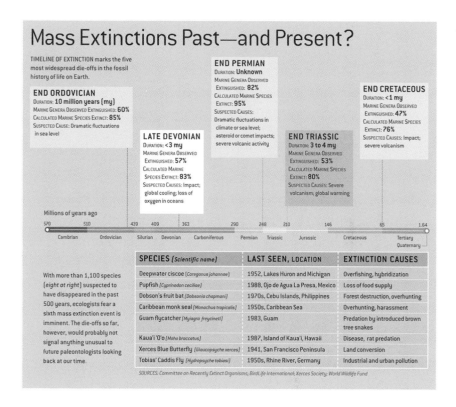

Mass Extinctions Past—and Present?

TIMELINE OF EXTINCTION marks the five most widespread die-offs in the fossil history of life on Earth.

END ORDOVICIAN
Duration: **10 million years (my)**
Marine Genera Observed Extinguished: **60%**
Calculated Marine Species Extinct: **85%**
Suspected Cause: Dramatic fluctuations in sea level

LATE DEVONIAN
Duration: **<3 my**
Marine Genera Observed Extinguished: **57%**
Calculated Marine Species Extinct: **83%**
Suspected Causes: Impact; global cooling; loss of oxygen in oceans

END PERMIAN
Duration: **Unknown**
Marine Genera Observed Extinguished: **82%**
Calculated Marine Species Extinct: **95%**
Suspected Causes: Dramatic fluctuations in climate or sea level; asteroid or comet impacts; severe volcanic activity

END TRIASSIC
Duration: **3 to 4 my**
Marine Genera Observed Extinguished: **53%**
Calculated Marine Species Extinct: **80%**
Suspected Causes: Severe volcanism; global warming

END CRETACEOUS
Duration: **<1 my**
Marine Genera Observed Extinguished: **47%**
Calculated Marine Species Extinct: **76%**
Suspected Causes: Impact; severe volcanism

Millions of years ago

| 570 | 510 | 439 | 409 | 363 | 290 | 248 | 210 | 146 | 65 | 1.64 |

| Cambrian | Ordovician | Silurian | Devonian | Carboniferous | Permian | Triassic | Jurassic | Cretaceous | Tertiary Quaternary |

With more than 1,100 species (eight at right) suspected to have disappeared in the past 500 years, ecologists fear a sixth mass extinction event is imminent. The die-offs so far, however, would probably not signal anything unusual to future paleontologists looking back at our time.

SPECIES (Scientific name)	LAST SEEN, LOCATION	EXTINCTION CAUSES
Deepwater ciscoe (Coregonus johannae)	1952, Lakes Huron and Michigan	Overfishing, hybridization
Pupfish (Cyprinodon ceciliae)	1988, Ojo de Agua La Presa, Mexico	Loss of food supply
Dobson's fruit bat (Dobsonia chapmani)	1970s, Cebu Islands, Philippines	Forest destruction, overhunting
Caribbean monk seal (Monachus tropicalis)	1950s, Caribbean Sea	Overhunting, harassment
Guam flycatcher (Myiagra freycineti)	1983, Guam	Predation by introduced brown tree snakes
Kaua'i 'O'o (Moho braccatus)	1987, Island of Kaua'i, Hawaii	Disease, rat predation
Xerces Blue Butterfly (Glaucopsyche xerces)	1941, San Francisco Peninsula	Land conversion
Tobias' Caddis Fly (Hydropsyche tobiasi)	1950s, Rhine River, Germany	Industrial and urban pollution

SOURCES: Committee on Recently Extinct Organisms; BirdLife International; Xerces Society; World Wildlife Fund

University of Århus, he alleges that environmentalists have ignored recent evidence that tropical deforestation is not taking the toll that was feared. "No well-investigated group of animals shows a pattern of loss that is consistent with greatly heightened extinction rates," MacPhee concurs. The best models, Lomborg suggests, project an extinction rate of 0.15 percent of species per decade, "not a catastrophe but a problem—one of many that mankind still needs to solve."

. . . or Gloom?

"It's a tough question to put numbers on," Wilson allows. May agrees but says "that isn't an argument for not asking the question" of whether a mass extinction event is upon us.

To answer that question, we need to know three things: the natural (or "background") extinction rate, the current rate and whether the pace of extinction is steady or changing. The first step, Wilson explains, is to work out the mean life span of a species from the fossil record. "The background extinction rate is then the inverse of that. If species are born at random and all live exactly one million years—and it varies, but it's on that order—then that means one species in a million naturally goes extinct each year," he says.

In a 1995 article that is still cited in almost every scientific paper on this subject (even in Lomborg's book), May used a similar method to compute the background rate. He relied on estimates that put the mean species life span at five million to 10 million years, however; he thus came up with a rate that is five to 10 times lower than Wilson's. But according to paleontologist David M. Raup (then at the University of Chicago), who published some of the figures May and Wilson relied on, their calculations are seriously flawed by three false assumptions.

One is that species of plants, mammals, insects, marine invertebrates and other groups all exist for about the same time. In fact, the typical survival time appears to vary among groups by a factor of 10 or more, with mammal species among the least durable. Second, they assume that all organisms have an equal chance of making it into the fossil record. But paleontologists estimate that fewer than 4 percent of all species that ever lived are preserved as fossils. "And the species we do see are the widespread, very successful ones," Raup says. "The weak species confined to some hilltop or island all went extinct before they could be fossilized," adds John Alroy of the University of California at Santa Barbara.

The third problem is that May and Wilson use an average life span when they should use a median. Because "the vast majority of species are short-lived," Raup says, "the average is distorted by the very few that have very long life spans." All three oversimplifications underestimate the background rate—and make the current picture scarier in comparison.

Earlier this year U.C.S.B. biomathematician Helen M. Regan and several of her colleagues published the first attempt ever to correct for the strong biases and uncertainties in the data. They looked exclusively at mammals, the best-studied group. They estimated how many of the mammals now living, and how many of those recently extinguished, would show up as fossils. They also factored in the uncertainty for each number rather than relying on best guesses. In the end they concluded that "the current rate of

The Portfolio of Life

How severe is the extinction crisis? That depends in large part on how many species there are altogether. The greater the number, the more species will die out every year from natural causes and the more new ones will naturally appear. But although the general outlines of the tree of life are clear, scientists are unsure how many twigs lie at the end of each branch. When it comes to bacteria, viruses, protists and archaea (a whole kingdom of single-celled life-forms discovered just a few decades ago), microbiologists have only vague notions of how many branches there are.

Birds, fish, mammals and plants are the exceptions. Sizing up the global workforce of about 5,000 professional taxonomists, zoologist Robert M. May of the University of Oxford noted that about equal numbers study vertebrates, plants and invertebrates. "You may wish to think this record reflects some judicious appreciation of what's important," he says.

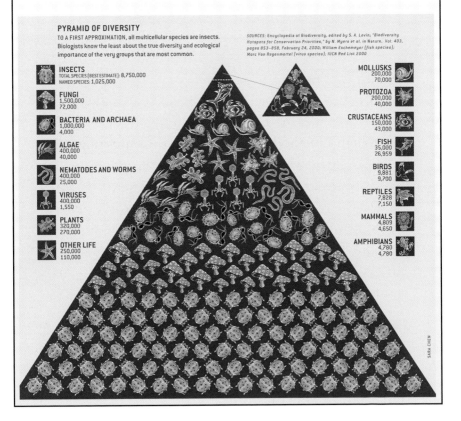

PYRAMID OF DIVERSITY
TO A FIRST APPROXIMATION, all multicellular species are insects. Biologists know the least about the true diversity and ecological importance of the very groups that are most common.

SOURCES: Encyclopedia of Biodiversity, edited by S. A. Levin; "Biodiversity Hotspots for Conservation Priorities," by N. Myers et al. in Nature, Vol. 403, pages 853–858, February 24, 2000; William Eschemeyer (fish species); Marc Van Regenmortel (virus species); IUCN Red List 2000

INSECTS
TOTAL SPECIES (BEST ESTIMATE): 8,750,000
NAMED SPECIES: 1,025,000

FUNGI
1,500,000
72,000

BACTERIA AND ARCHAEA
1,000,000
4,000

ALGAE
400,000
40,000

NEMATODES AND WORMS
400,000
25,000

VIRUSES
400,000
1,550

PLANTS
320,000
270,000

OTHER LIFE
250,000
110,000

MOLLUSKS
200,000
70,000

PROTOZOA
200,000
40,000

CRUSTACEANS
150,000
43,000

FISH
35,000
26,959

BIRDS
9,881
9,700

REPTILES
7,828
7,150

MAMMALS
4,809
4,650

AMPHIBIANS
4,780
4,780

SARA CHEN

"My view of that is: absolute garbage. Whether you are interested in how ecosystems evolved, their current functioning or how they are likely to respond to climate change, you're going to learn a lot more by looking at soil microorganisms than at charismatic vertebrates."

For every group except birds, says Peter Hammond of the National History Museum in London, new species are now being discovered faster than ever before, thanks to several new international projects. An All Taxa Biodiversity Inventory under way in Great Smoky Mountains National Park in North Carolina and Tennessee has discovered 115 species—80 percent of them insects or arachnids—in its first 18 months of work. Last year 40 scientists formed the All Species Project, a society devoted to the (probably quixotic) goal of cataloguing every living species, microbes included, within 25 years.

Other projects, such as the Global Biodiversity Information Facility and Species2000, are building Internet databases that will codify species records that are now scattered among the world's museums and universities. If biodiversity is defined in strictly pragmatic terms as the variety of life-forms we know about, it is growing prodigiously.

mammalian extinction lies between 17 and 377 times the background extinction rate." The best estimate, they wrote, is a 36- to 78-fold increase.

Regan's method is still imperfect. Comparing the past 400 years with the previous 65 million unavoidably assumes, she says, "that the current extinction rate will be sustained over millions of years." Alroy recently came up with a way to measure the speed of extinctions that doesn't suffer from such assumptions. Over the past 200 years, he figures, the rate of loss among mammal species has been some 120 times higher than natural.

A Grim Guessing Game

Attempts to figure out the current extinction rate are fraught with even more uncertainties. The international conservation organization IUCN keeps "Red Lists" of organisms suspected to be extinct in the wild. But MacPhee complains that "the IUCN methodology for recognizing extinction is not sufficiently rigorous to be reliable." He and other extinction experts have formed the Committee on Recently Extinct Organisms, which combed the Red Lists to identify those species that were clearly unique and that had not been found despite a reasonable search. They certified 60 of the 87 mammals listed by IUCN as extinct but claim that only 33 of the 92 freshwater fish presumed extinct by IUCN are definitely gone forever.

For every species falsely presumed absent, however, there may be hundreds or thousands that vanish unknown to science. "We are uncertain to a factor of 10 about how many species we share the planet with," May points out. "My guess would be roughly seven million, but credible guesses range from five to 15 million," excluding microorganisms.

Taxonomists have named approximately 1.8 million species, but biologists know almost nothing about most of them, especially the insects, nematodes and crustaceans that dominate the animal kingdom. Some 40 percent of the 400,000 known beetle species have each been recorded at just one location—and with no idea of individual species' range, scientists have no way to confirm its extinction. Even invertebrates known to be extinct often go unrecorded: when the passenger pigeon was eliminated in 1914, it took two species of parasitic lice with it. They still do not appear on IUCN's list.

"It is extremely difficult to observe an extinction; it's like seeing an airplane crash," Wilson says. Not that scientists aren't trying. Articles on the "biotic holocaust," as Myers calls it, usually figure that the vast majority of extinctions have been in the tropical Americas. Freshwater fishes are especially vulnerable, with more than a quarter listed as threatened. "I work in Venezuela, which has substantially more freshwater fishes than all of North America. After 30 years of work, we've done a reasonable job of cataloguing fish diversity there," observes Winemiller of Texas A&M, "yet we can't point to one documented case of extinction."

A similar pattern emerges for other groups of organisms, he claims. "If you are looking for hard evidence of tens or hundreds or thousands of species disappearing each year, you aren't going to find it. That could be because the database is woefully inadequate," he acknowledges. "But one shouldn't dismiss the possibility that it's not going to be the disaster everyone fears."

The Logic of Loss

The disaster scenarios are based on several independent lines of evidence that seem to point to fast and rising extinction rates. The most widely accepted is the species-area relation. "Generally speaking, as the area of habitat falls, the number of species living in it drops proportionally by the third root to the sixth root," explains Wilson, who first deduced this equation more than 30 years ago. "A middle value is the fourth root, which means that when you eliminate 90 percent of the habitat, the number of species falls by half."

"From that rough first estimate and the rate of the destruction of the tropical forest, which is about 1 percent a year," Wilson continues, "we can predict that about one quarter of 1 percent of species either become extinct immediately or are doomed to much earlier extinction." From a pool of roughly 10 million species, we should thus expect about 25,000 to evaporate annually.

Extinction Filters

Survival of the fittest takes on a new meaning when humans develop a region. Among four Mediterranean climate regions, those developed more recently have lost larger fractions of their vascular plant species in modern times. Once the species least compatible with agriculture are filtered out by "artificial selection," extinction rates seem to fall.

REGION (in order of development	EXTINCT (per 1,000)	THREATENED (percent)
Mediterranean	1.3	14.7
South African Cape	3.0	15.2
California	4.0	10.2
Western Australia	6.6	17.5

SOURCE: "Extinctions in Mediterranean Areas." Werner Greuter in Extinction Rates. Edited by J. H. Lawton and R. H. May. Oxford University Press, 1995

Lomborg challenges that view on three grounds, however. Species-area relations were worked out by comparing the number of species on islands and do not necessarily apply to fragmented habitats on the mainland. "More than half of Costa Rica's native bird species occur in largely deforested countryside habitats, together with similar fractions of mammals and butterflies," Stanford University biologist Gretchen Daily noted recently in *Nature*. Although they may not thrive, a large fraction of forest species may survive on farmland and in woodlots—for how long, no one yet knows.

That would help explain Lomborg's second observation, which is that in both the eastern U.S. and Puerto Rico, clearance of more than 98 percent of the primary forests did not wipe out half of the bird species in them. Four centuries of logging "resulted in the extinction of only one forest bird" out of 200 in the U.S. and seven out of 60 native species in Puerto Rico, he asserts.

Such criticisms misunderstand the species-area theory, according to Stuart L. Pimm of Columbia University. "Habitat destruction acts like a cookie cutter stamping out poorly mixed dough," he wrote last year in *Nature*. "Species found only within the stamped-out area are themselves stamped out. Those found more widely are not."

Of the 200 bird types in the forests of the eastern U.S., Pimm states, all but 28 also lived elsewhere. Moreover, the forest was cleared gradually, and gradually it regrew as farmland was abandoned. So even at the low point, around 1872, woodland covered half the extent of the original forest. The species-area theory predicts that a 50 percent reduction should knock out 16 percent of the endemic species: in this case, four birds. And four species did go extinct. Lomborg discounts one of those four that may have been a subspecies and two others that perhaps succumbed to unrelated insults.

But even if the species-area equation holds, Lomborg responds, official statistics suggest that deforestation has been slowing and is now well below 1 percent a year. The U.N. Food and Agriculture Organization recently estimated that from 1990 to 2000 the world's forest cover dropped at an average annual rate of 0.2 percent (11.5 million hectares felled, minus 2.5 million hectares of new growth).

Annual forest loss was around half a percent in most of the tropics, however, and that is where the great majority of rare and threatened species live. So although "forecasters may get these figures wrong now and then, perhaps colored by a desire to sound the alarm, this is just a matter of timescale," replies Carlos A. Peres, a Brazilian ecologist at the University of East Anglia in England.

An Uncertain Future

Ecologists have tried other means to project future extinction rates. May and his co-workers watched how vertebrate species moved through the threat categories in IUCN's database over a four-year period (two years for plants), projected those very small numbers far into the future and concluded that extinction rates will rise 12- to 55-fold over the next 300 years. Georgina M. Mace, director of science at the Zoological Society of London, came to a similar conclusion by combining models that plot survival odds for a few very well known species. Entomologist Nigel E. Stork of the Natural History Museum in London noted that a British bird is 10 times more likely than a British bug to be endangered. He then extrapolated such ratios to the rest of the world to predict 100,000 to 500,000 insect extinctions by 2300. Lomborg favors this latter model, from which he concludes that "the rate for all animals will remain below 0.208 percent per decade and probably be below 0.7 percent per 50 years."

It takes a heroic act of courage for any scientist to erect such long and broad projections on such a thin and lopsided base of data. Especially when, according to May, the data on endangered species "may tell us more about the vagaries of sampling efforts, of taxonomists' interests and of data entry than about the real changes in species' status."

Biologists have some good theoretical reasons to fear that even if mass extinction hasn't begun yet, collapse is imminent. At the conference in Hilo, Kevin Higgins of the University of Oregon presented a computer model that tracks artificial organisms in a population, simulating their genetic mutation rates, reproductive behavior and ecological interactions. He found that "in small populations, mutations tend to be mild enough that natural selection doesn't filter them out. That dramatically shortens the time to extinction." So as habitats shrink and populations are wiped out—at a rate of perhaps 16 million a year, Daily has estimated—"this could be a time bomb, an extinction event occurring under the surface," Higgins warns. But proving that that bomb is ticking in the wild will not be easy.

And what will happen to fig trees, the most widespread plant genus in the tropics, if it loses the single parasitic wasp variety that pollinates every one of its 900 species? Or to the 79 percent of canopy-level trees in the Samoan rain forests if hunters kill off the flying foxes on which they depend? Part of the reason so many conservationists are so fearful is that they expect the arches of entire ecosystems to fall once a few "keystone" species are removed.

Others distrust that metaphor. "Several recent studies seem to show that there is some redundancy in ecosystems," says Melodie A. McGeoch of the University of Pretoria in South Africa, although she cautions that what is redundant today may not be redundant tomorrow. "It really doesn't make sense to think the majority of species would go down with marginally higher pressures than if humans weren't on the scene," MacPhee adds. "Evolution should make them resilient."

If natural selection doesn't do so, artificial selection might, according to work by Werner Greuter of the Free University of Berlin, Thomas M. Brooks of Conservation International and others. Greuter compared the rate of recent plant extinctions in four ecologically similar regions and discovered that the longest-settled, most disturbed area—the Mediterranean—had the lowest rate. Plant extinction rates were higher in California and South Africa, and they were highest in Western Australia. The solution to this apparent paradox, they propose, is that species that cannot coexist with human land use tend to die out soon after agriculture begins. Those that are left are better equipped to dodge the darts we throw at them. Human-induced extinctions may thus fall over time.

If true, that has several implications. Millennia ago our ancestors may have killed off many more species than we care to think about in Europe, Asia and other long-settled regions. On the other hand, we may have more time than we fear to prevent future catastrophes in areas where humans have been part of the ecosystem for a while—and less time than we hope to avoid them in what little wilderness remains pristine.

"The question is how to deal with uncertainty, because there really is no way to make that uncertainty go away," Winemiller argues. "We think the situation is extremely serious; we just don't think the species extinction issue is the peg the conservation movement should hang its hat on. Otherwise, if it turns out to be wrong, where does that leave us?"

Long-Term Savings
It could leave conservationists with less of a sense of urgency and with a handful of weak political and

Why Biodiversity Doesn't (Yet) Pay

Foz do Iguaçu, Brazil—At the International Congress of Entomologists last summer, Ebbe Nielsen, director of the Australian National Insect Collection in Canberra, reflected on the reasons why, despite the 1992 Convention on Biological Diversity signed here in Brazil by 178 countries, so little has happened since to secure the world's threatened species. "You and I can say extinction rates are too high and we have to stop it, but to convince the politicians we have to have convincing reasons," he said. "In developing countries, the economic pressures are so high, people use whatever they can find today to survive until tomorrow. As long as that's the case, there will be no support for biodiversity at all."

Not, that is, unless it can be made more profitable to leave a forest standing or a wetland wet than it is to convert the land to farm, pasture or parking lot. Unfortunately, time has not been kind to the several arguments environmentalists have made to assign economic value to each one of perhaps 10 million species.

A Hedge against Disease and Famine

"Narrowly utilitarian arguments say: The incredible genetic diversity contained in the population and species diversity that we are heirs to is ultimately the raw stuff of tomorrow's biotechnological revolution," observes Robert May of Oxford. "It is the source of new drugs." Or new foods, adds E. O. Wilson of Harvard, should something happen to the 30 crops that supply 90 percent of the calories to the human diet, or to the 14 animal species that make up 90 percent of our livestock.

"Some people who say that may even believe it," May continues. "I don't. Give us 20 or 30 years and we will design new drugs from the molecule up, as we are already beginning to do."

Hopes were raised 10 years ago by reports that Merck had paid $1.14 million to InBio, a Costa Rican conservation group, for novel chemicals extracted from rainforest species. The contract would return royalties to InBio if any of the leads became drugs. But none have, and Merck terminated the agreement in 1999. Shaman Pharmaceuticals, founded in 1989 to commercialize traditional medicinal plants, got as far as late-stage clinical trials but then went bankrupt. And given, as Wilson himself notes in The Diversity of Life, that more than 90 percent of the known varieties of the basic food plants are on deposit in seed banks, national parks are hardly the cheapest form of insurance against crop failures.

Ecosystem Services

"Potentially the strongest argument," May says, "is a broadly utilitarian one: ecological systems deliver services we're only just beginning to think of trying to estimate. We do not understand how much you can simplify these systems and yet still have them function. As Aldo Leopold once said, the first rule of intelligent tinkering is to keep all the pieces."

The trouble with this argument, explains Columbia University economist Geoffrey Heal, is that "it does not make sense to ask about the value of replacing a life-support system." Economics can only assign values to things for which there are markets, he says. If all oil were to vanish, for example, we could switch to alternative fuels that cost $50 a barrel. But that does not determine the price of oil.

And although recent experiments suggest that removing a large fraction of species from a small area lowers its biomass and ability to soak up carbon dioxide, scientists cannot say yet whether the principle applies to whole ecosystems. "It may be that a grievously simplified world—the world of the cult movie *Blade Runner*—can be so run that we can survive in it," May concedes.

A Duty of Stewardship

Because science knows so little of the millions of species out there, let alone what complex roles each one plays in the ecosystems it inhabits, it may never be possible for economics to come to the aid of endangered species. A moral argument may thus be the best last hope—certainly it is appeals to leaders' sense of stewardship that have accomplished the most so far. But is it hazardous for scientists to make it?

They do, of course, in various forms. To Wilson, "a species is a masterpiece of evolution, a million-year-old entity encoded by five billion genetic letters, exquisitely adapted to the niche it inhabits." For that reason, conservation biologist David Ehrenfeld proposed in *The Arrogance of Humanism*, "long-standing existence in Nature is deemed to carry with it the unimpeachable right to continued existence."

Winning public recognition of such a right will take much education and persuasion. According to a poll last year, fewer than one quarter of Americans recognized the term "biological diversity." Three quarters expressed concern about species and habitat loss, but that is down from 87 percent in 1996. And May observes that the concept of biodiversity stewardship "is a developed-world luxury. If we were in abject poverty trying to put food in the mouth of the fifth child, the argument would have less resonance."

But if scientists "proselytize on behalf of biodiversity"—as Wilson, Lovejoy, Ehrlich and many others have done—they should realize that "such work carries perils," advises David Takacs of California State University at Monterey Bay. "Advocacy threatens to undermine the perception of value neutrality and objectivity that leads laypersons to listen to scientists in the first place." And yet if those who know rare species best and love them most cannot speak openly on their behalf, who will?

economic arguments [see "Why Diversity Doesn't (Yet) Pay" box]. It might also force them to realize that "many of the species in trouble today are in fact already members of the doomed, living dead," as David S. Woodruff wrote in the *Proceedings of the National Academy of Sciences* this past May. "Triage" is a dirty word to many environmentalists. "Unless we say no species loss is acceptable, then we have no line in the sand to defend, and we will be pushed back and back as losses build," Brooks argued at the Hilo meeting. But losses are inevitable, Wilson says, until the human population stops growing.

"I call that the bottleneck," Wilson elaborates, "because we have to pass through that scramble for remaining resources in order to get to an era, perhaps sometime in the 22nd century, of declining population. Our goal is to carry as much of the biodiversity through as possible." Biologists are divided, however, on whether the few charismatic species now recognized as endangered should determine what gets pulled through the bottleneck.

"The argument that when you protect birds and mammals, the other things come with them just doesn't stand up to close examination," May says. A smarter goal is "to try to conserve the greatest amount of evolutionary history." Far more valuable than a panda or rhino, he suggests, are relic life-forms such as the tuatara, a large iguanalike reptile that lives only on islets off the coast of New Zealand. Just two species of tuatara remain from a group that branched off from the main stem of the reptilian evolutionary tree so long ago that this couple make up a genus, an order and almost a subclass all by themselves.

But Woodruff, who is an ecologist at the University of California at San Diego, invokes an even broader principle. "Some of us advocate a shift from saving things, the products of evolution, to saving the underlying process, evolution itself," he writes. "This process will ultimately provide us with the most cost-effective solution to the general problem of conserving nature."

There are still a few large areas where natural selection alone determines which species succeed and which fail. "Why not save functioning ecosystems that haven't been despoiled yet?" Winemiller asks. "Places like the Guyana shield region of South America contain far more species than some of the so-called hotspots." To do so would mean purchasing tracts large enough to accommodate entire ecosystems as they roll north and south in response to the shifting climate. It would also mean prohibiting all human uses of the land. It may not be impossible: utterly undeveloped wilderness is relatively cheap, and the population of potential buyers has recently exploded.

"It turns out to be a lot easier to persuade a corporate CEO or a billionaire of the importance of the issue than it is to convince the American public," Wilson says. "With a Ted Turner or a Gordon Moore or a Craig McCaw involved, you can accomplish almost as much as a government of a developed country would with a fairly generous appropriation."

"Maybe even more," agrees Richard E. Rice, chief economist for Conservation International. With money from Moore, McCaw, Turner and other donors, CI has outcompeted logging companies for forested land in Suriname and Guyana. In Bolivia, Rice reports, "we conserved an area the size of Rhode Island for half the price of a house in my neighborhood," and the Nature Conservancy was able to have a swath of rain forest as big as Yellowstone National Park set aside for a mere $1.5 million. In late July, Peru issued to an environmental group the country's first "conservation concession"—essentially a renewable lease for the right to *not* develop the land—for 130,000 hectares of forest. Peru has now opened some 60 million hectares of its public forests to such concessions, Rice says. And efforts are under way to negotiate similar deals in Guatemala and Cameroon.

"Even without massive support in public opinion or really effective government policy in the U.S., things are turning upward," Wilson says, with a look of cautious optimism on his face. Perhaps it is a bit early to despair after all.

More to Explore

Extinction Rates. Edited by John H. Lawton and
    Robert M. May. Oxford University Press, 1995.
The Currency and Tempo of Extinction. Helen M.
    Regan et al. in the *American Naturalist*, Vol. 157,
    No. 1, pages 1–10; January 2001.

Encyclopedia of Biodiversity. Edited by Simon Asher Levin. Academic Press, 2001.

The Skeptical Environmentalist. Bjørn Lomborg. Cambridge University Press, 2001.

About the Author

W. WAYT GIBBS is senior writer.

"Cloning
2. Noah's Ark"

By Robert P. Lanza, Betsy L. Dresser and
Philip Damiani

*Biotechnology might offer the best way to keep some endangered species
from disappearing from the planet.*

In late November a humble Iowa cow is slated to give
birth to the world's first cloned endangered species, a
baby bull to be named Noah. Noah is a gaur: a member
of a species of large oxlike animals that are now rare
in their homelands of India, Indochina and southeast
Asia. These one-ton bovines have been hunted for sport
for generations. More recently the gaur's habitats of
forests, bamboo jungles and grasslands have dwindled to
the point that only roughly 36,000 are thought to remain
in the wild. The World Conservation Union–IUCN Red
Data Book lists the gaur as endangered, and trade in
live gaur or gaur products—whether horns, hides or
hooves—is banned by the Convention on International
Trade in Endangered Species (CITES).

But if all goes as predicted, in a few weeks a
spindly-legged little Noah will trot in a new day in the
conservation of his kind as well as in the preservation
of many other endangered species. Perhaps most important, he will be living, mooing proof that one animal
can carry and give birth to the exact genetic duplicate,
or clone, of an animal of a different species. And Noah

will be just the first creature up the ramp of the ark of endangered species that we and other scientists are currently attempting to clone: plans are under way to clone the African bongo antelope, the Sumatran tiger and that favorite of zoo lovers, the reluctant-to-reproduce giant panda. Cloning could also reincarnate some species that are already extinct—most immediately, perhaps, the bucardo mountain goat of Spain. The last bucardo— a female—died of a smashed skull when a tree fell on it early this year, but Spanish scientists have preserved some of its cells.

Advances in cloning offer a way to preserve and propagate endangered species that reproduce poorly in zoos until their habitats can be restored and they can be reintroduced to the wild. Cloning's main power, however, is that it allows researchers to introduce new genes back into the gene pool of a species that has few remaining animals. Most zoos are not equipped to collect and cryopreserve semen; similarly, eggs are difficult to obtain and are damaged by freezing. But by cloning animals whose body cells have been preserved, scientists can keep the genes of that individual alive, maintaining (and in some instances increasing) the overall genetic diversity of endangered populations of that species.

Nevertheless, some conservation biologists have been slow to recognize the benefits of basic assisted reproduction strategies, such as in vitro fertilization, and have been hesitant to consider cloning. Although we agree that every effort should be made to preserve wild spaces for the incredible diversity of life that inhabits this planet, in some cases either the battle has already been lost or its outcome looks dire. Cloning technology is not a panacea, but it offers the opportunity to save some of the species that contribute to that diversity. A clone still requires a mother, however, and very few conservationists would advocate rounding up wild female endangered animals for that purpose or subjecting a precious zoo resident of the same species to the rigors of assisted reproduction and surrogate motherhood. That means that to clone an endangered species, researchers such as ourselves must solve the problem of how to get cells from two different species to yield the clone of one.

A Gaur Is Born

It is a deceptively simple-looking process. A needle jabs through the protective layer, or zona pellucida, surrounding an egg that hours ago resided in a living ovary. In one deft movement, a research assistant uses it to suck out the egg's nucleus—which contains the majority of a cell's genetic material—leaving behind only a sac of gel called cytoplasm. Next he uses a second needle to inject another, whole cell under the egg's outer layer. With the flip of an electric switch, the cloning is complete: the electrical pulse fuses the introduced cell to the egg, and the early embryo begins to divide. In a few days, it will become a mass of cells large enough

The Nuclear Transfer (Cloning) Process

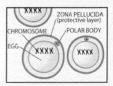

Recipient eggs are coaxed to mature in a culture dish. Each has a remnant egg cell called the polar body.

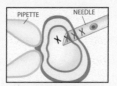

The polar bodies and chromosomes of each egg are drawn into a needle. A pipette holds the egg still.

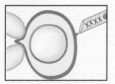

Once the chromosomes and polar body are removed, all that remains inside the zona pellucida is cytoplasm.

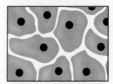

Skin cells called fibroblasts are isolated from the animal to be cloned and grown in culture dishes.

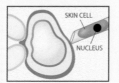

An entire skin cell is taken up into the needle, which is again punched through the zona pellucida.

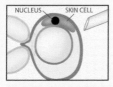

The skin cell is injected underneath the zona pellucida, where it remains separate from the egg cytoplasm.

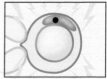

Each injected egg is exposed to an electric shock that fuses the skin cell with the egg cytoplasm.

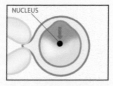

The skin cell's nucleus, with its genes, enters the egg cytoplasm. Within a few hours, the fused cell begins to divide.

to implant into the uterus of a surrogate-mother animal previously treated with hormones. In a matter of months, that surrogate mother will give birth to a clone.

In practice, though, this technique—which scientists call nuclear transfer—is not so easy. To create Noah, we at Advanced Cell Technology (ACT) in Worcester, Mass., had to fuse skin cells taken from a male gaur with 692 enucleated cow eggs. As we report in the current issue of the journal *Cloning*, of those 692 cloned early embryos, only 81 grew in the laboratory into blastocysts, balls of 100 or so cells that are sufficiently developed to implant for gestation. We ended up inserting 42 blastocysts into 32 cows, but only eight became pregnant. We removed the fetuses from two of the pregnant cows for scientific analysis; four other animals experienced spontaneous abortions in the second or third month of the usual nine-month pregnancy; and the seventh cow had a very unexpected late-term spontaneous abortion in August.

The statistics of the efficiency of cloning reflect the fact that the technology is still as much an art as it is a science—particularly when it involves transplanting an embryo into another species. Scientists, including those of us at ACT, have had the highest success rates cloning domestic cattle implanted into cows of the same species. But even in this instance we have had to work hard to produce just a few animals. For every 100 cow eggs we fuse with adult cattle cells, we can expect only between 15 and 20 to produce blastocysts. And only roughly 10 percent of those—one or two—yield live births.

The numbers reflect difficulties with the nuclear transfer process itself, which we are now working to understand. They are also a function of the vagaries of assisted reproduction technology.

Accordingly, we expect that the first few endangered species to be cloned will be those whose reproduction has already been well studied. Several zoos and conservation societies—including the Audubon Institute Center for Research of Endangered Species (AICRES) in New Orleans, which is led by one of us (Dresser)—have probed the reproductive biology of a range of endangered species, with some notable successes. Last November, for example, Dresser and her colleagues reported the first transplantation of a previously frozen embryo of an endangered animal into another species that resulted in a live birth. In this case, an ordinary house cat gave birth to an African wildcat, a species that has declined in some areas.

So far, beyond the African wildcat and the gaur, we and others have accomplished interspecies embryo transfers in four additional cases: an Indian desert cat into a domestic cat; a bongo antelope into a more common African antelope called an eland; a mouflon sheep into a domestic sheep; and a rare red deer into a common white-tailed deer. All yielded live births. We hope that the studies of felines will pave the way for cloning the cheetah, of which only roughly 12,000 remain in southern Africa. The prolonged courtship behavior of cheetahs requires substantial territory, a possible explanation for why the animals have bred so poorly in zoos and yet another reason to fear their extinction as their habitat shrinks.

Panda-monium

One of the most exciting candidates for endangered-species cloning—the giant panda—has not yet been the subject of interspecies transfer experiments, but it has benefited from assisted reproduction technology. Following the well-publicized erotic fumblings of the National Zoo's ill-fated panda pair, the late Ling-Ling and Hsing-Hsing, the San Diego Zoo turned to artificial insemination to make proud parents of its Bai Yun and Shi Shi. Baby Hua Mei was born in August 1999.

Giant pandas are such emblems of endangered species that the World Wildlife Fund (WWF) uses one in its logo. According to a census that is now almost 20 years old, fewer than 1,000 pandas remain in their mountainous habitats of bamboo forest in southwest China. But some biologists think that the population might have rebounded a bit in some areas. The WWF expects to complete a census of China's pandas in mid-2002 to produce a better estimate.

In the meantime, we at ACT are discussing plans with the government of China to clone a giant panda. Chinese scientists have already made strides toward the goal of panda cloning. In August 1999 Dayuan Chen of the institute and his co-workers published a paper in the English-language journal *Science in China* announcing that they had fused panda skeletal muscle, uterus and mammary gland cells with the eggs of a rabbit and then coaxed the cloned cells to develop into blastocysts in the laboratory.

A rabbit, of course, is too small to serve as a surrogate mother for a giant panda. Instead ACT and the Chinese plan to turn to American black bears. As this issue of *Scientific American* goes to press, ACT is finalizing plans to obtain eggs from female black bears killed during this autumn's hunting season in the northeastern U.S. Together with the Chinese, ACT scientists hope to use these eggs and frozen cells from the late Hsing-Hsing or Ling-Ling to generate cloned giant panda embryos that can be implanted into a female black bear now living in a zoo. A research group that includes veterinarians at Bear Country U.S.A. in Rapid City, S.D., has already demonstrated that black bears can give birth to transplanted embryos. They reported the successful birth of a black bear cub from an embryo transferred from one pregnant black bear to another last year in the journal *Theriogenology*.

AICRES scientists hope to take advantage of the success with bongo antelope that one of us (Dresser) had while at the Cincinnati Zoo. In 1984 Dresser and Charles Earle Pope of the University of Alabama at Birmingham (now with AICRES and Louisiana State University) and their colleagues announced the birth of a bongo after moving very early embryos from a pregnant female bongo to an eland surrogate mother.

Most of the mountain subspecies of bongo—a medium-size antelope with vertical white stripes—live in captivity. According to the World Conservation Union–IUCN, the mountain bongo is endangered, with only 50 or so remaining in a small region of Kenya. In contrast, the 1999 Bongo International Studbook lists nearly 550 mountain bongo living in zoos throughout the world. The lowland bongo subspecies is slightly

What About Rover and Fluffy?

The list of domesticated animals that scientists have been able to clone so far includes sheep, cattle, goats and laboratory mice—and now, we expect, the gaur. Compared with that menagerie, you'd think that cloning an ordinary dog or cat would be a snap. Unfortunately, this has not been the case. Both of our research groups have created cloned cat embryos and have implanted them into female cats, but as this article goes to press, neither of our teams has yet obtained a full-term pregnancy. Dogs have presented even more problems.

But we anticipate success soon. At Advanced Cell Technology (ACT), we have undertaken a research program that uses cloning technology to propagate pets as well as service animals such as seeing-eye dogs for the blind, hearing dogs for the deaf, search-and-rescue dogs, and animals used for social therapy. Together with Louisiana State University, the Audubon Institute has teamed up with a company called Lazaron BioTechnologies in Baton Rouge, La., to clone pet dogs and cats.

A surprising number of people are interested in cloning their favorite deceased pet in the hope of getting an animal with similar behavioral characteristics. A good deal of a cat or dog's demeanor is thought to be genetically determined. Although one can argue that there are already plenty of cats and dogs in the world that need homes, people still use traditional breeding methods to try to reproduce a particularly desirable animal. Cloning could offer a more efficient alternative. It could be particularly important in the case of service animals. Currently, for instance, male seeing-eye dogs are neutered at an early age so that they can concentrate better during their expensive and rigorous training. So, unfortunately, even if a dog turns out to be very good at his job, he can't be bred to produce more like him.

Our efforts to clone pets could also pay off for endangered species. We expect to be able to apply the information we obtain from cloning cats and dogs to preserving endangered felines and canines.

ACT and several other companies now offer pet cloning kits that veterinarians can use to preserve samples from a client's pet for possible future cloning. The kits contain materials for collecting a skin specimen and sending it back to a laboratory. Research assistants there use the tissue to establish a collection of pure, dividing cells called a cell line, which will be the source of donor cells for cloning.

ACT extracts eggs for the cloning procedure from reproductive tracts taken from animals that have been spayed by veterinarians. We remove the ovaries and carefully puncture all visible follicles to release the eggs. Then we collect the eggs and place them in a specialized maturation medium that contains hormones, proteins and nutrients. Once fully matured, the eggs are ready for the nuclear transfer procedure [see "The Nuclear Transfer (Cloning) Process" illustration].

So far our main focus has been the domestic cat, primarily because its reproductive physiology has been well studied, and embryo transfers of early- and late-stage embryos have resulted in the birth of live kittens. Both ACT and the Audubon Institute have been able to establish systems for prompting cat eggs to mature in the lab and have consistently produced cloned embryos that are being transferred to recipients.

But dogs are a different story. The dog's reproductive physiology is unique among mammalian species. Dogs ovulate an immature egg that has a very long maturation time. This means that we need a different maturation system from the one we have used in cats and that we have fewer eggs to work with in the end. So Fluffy will probably have a leg up on Rover when it comes to cloning. —R.P.L., B.L.D. and P.D.

better off: it is listed as "near threatened" and has a population of perhaps several thousand scattered throughout central and western Africa.

A coalition of conservation organizations in the U.S. and Kenya is now planning to send mountain bongo that have been bred in captivity to two sites in Kenya. And in a new approach to reintroducing a species, AICRES is working in Kenya to transfer frozen bongo embryos into eland surrogates. Cloning could support these efforts and possibly yield more bongo for reintroduction.

But what about animals that are already extinct? Chances are slim to nil that scientists will soon be able to clone dinosaurs, à la *Jurassic Park*, or woolly mammoths. The primary problem is the dearth of preserved tissue— and hence DNA. A group of researchers unearthed what they had hoped would be a well-preserved mammoth last year, but repeated freezing and thawing over the eons had poked holes in the creature's DNA, and molecular biologists have not yet found a feasible way of filling in such genetic gaps.

A similar difficulty has hobbled efforts by Australian scientists to clone a thylacine, or Tasmanian tiger, a wolflike marsupial that died out in the 1930s. Researchers at the Australian Museum in Sydney are attempting to clone cells from a thylacine pup that was preserved in alcohol in 1866, but the DNA is in such poor condition that they say they will have to reconstruct all of the animal's chromosomes.

The recently extinct bucardo may prove a more promising target for resurrection. ACT is arranging a collaboration with Alberto Fernández-Arias and José Folch of the Agricultural Research Service in Zaragoza, Spain. Fernández-Arias froze tissue from the last bucardo. He and Folch had tried for several years to preserve the mountain goat, which in the end was wiped out by poaching, habitat destruction and landslides. Last year they transferred embryos from a subspecies related to the bucardo to a domestic goat, yielding live kids.

But even if interspecies nuclear transfer succeeds for the bucardo, it will yield only a sorority of clones, because we have tissue from just one animal, a female. ACT plans to try to make a male by removing one copy of the X chromosome from one of the female bucardo's cells and using a tiny artificial cell called a microsome to add a Y chromosome from a closely related goat species. The technology has been used by other researchers to manipulate human chromosomes, but it has never before been used for cloning. A nonprofit organization called the Soma Foundation has been established to help fund such efforts.

Why Clone?

Cloning endangered species is controversial, but we assert that it has an important place in plans to manage species that are in danger of extinction. Some researchers have argued against it, maintaining that it would restrict an already dwindling amount of genetic diversity for those species. Not so. We advocate the establishment of a worldwide network of repositories to hold frozen tissue from all the individuals of an endangered species from which it is possible to collect samples. Those cells—like the sperm and eggs now being collected in "frozen zoos" by a variety of zoological parks— could serve as a genetic trust for reconstituting entire populations of a given species. Such an enterprise would be relatively inexpensive: a typical three-foot freezer can hold more than 2,000 samples and uses just a few dollars of electricity per year. Currently only AICRES and the San Diego Zoo's Center for Reproduction of Endangered Species maintain banks of frozen body cells that could be used for cloning.

Other critics claim that the practice could over-shadow efforts to preserve habitat. We counter that while habitat preservation is the keystone of species conservation, some countries are too poor or too unstable to support sustainable conservation efforts. What is more, the continued growth of the human species will probably make it impossible to save enough habitat for some other species. Cloning by interspecies nuclear transfer offers the possibility of keeping the genetic stock of those species on hand without maintaining populations in captivity, which is a particularly costly enterprise in the case of large animals.

Another argument against cloning endangered species is that it might siphon donor money away from habitat maintenance. But not all potential donors are willing to support efforts to stem the tide of habitat destruction. We should recognize that some who would otherwise not donate to preserve endangered species at all might want to support cloning or other assisted reproduction technologies.

The time to act is now.

Further Information

Preservation of Endangered Species and Populations: A Role for Genome Banking, Somatic Cell Cloning, and Androgenesis? Graham E. Corley-Smith and Bruce P. Brandhorst in *Molecular Reproduction and Development*, Vol. 53, No. 3, pages 363–367; July 1999.

Biodiversity Hotspots for Conservation Priorities. Norman Myers, Russell A. Mittermeier, Cristina G. Mittermeier, Gustavo A. B. da Fonseca and Jennifer Kent in *Nature*, Vol. 403, No. 6772, pages 853–858; February 24, 2000.

Vanishing Before Our Eyes. E. O. Wilson in *Time*
(special report on Earth Day 2000), pages 29–34;
April–May 2000.

About the Authors

ROBERT P. LANZA, BETSY L. DRESSER and
PHILIP DAMIANI share an interest in reproductive
biology and animals. Lanza is vice president of medical
and scientific development at Advanced Cell Technology
(ACT) in Worcester, Mass. He founded the South
Meadow Pond and Wildlife Association in Worcester
County and is a member of the conservation commission of Clinton Township. Dresser is senior vice
president for research at the Audubon Institute and
director of the Audubon Institute Center for Research
of Endangered Species and the Freeport-McMoRan
Audubon Species Survival Center, all in New
Orleans. Damiani, a research scientist at ACT, is
also a member of the International Embryo Transfer
Society's committee on cryopreservation.

"Rethinking
3. Green Consumerism"

By Jared Hardner and Richard Rice

*Buying green products won't be enough to save biodiversity in the tropics.
A new plan for marketing conservation services may be the answer.*

Over the past decade, one popular tropical conservation effort has been to encourage consumers to pay
more for products that are cultivated or harvested in
ecologically sensitive ways. Myriad international
development projects have promoted these so-called
sustainable practices in forests and farms around the
world. Ordinary citizens in the U.S. and Europe
participate by choosing to buy timber, coffee and
other agricultural goods that are certified as having
met such special standards during production. One of
the best known of these certified, or "green," products
is shade-grown coffee beans, which are cultivated in
the shady forest understory rather than in sunny fields
where all the trees have been cut down.

Efforts to develop green products deserve support
and praise. But in the context of the global economy,
sustainable agriculture and consumer actions alone
will not be enough to conserve the plants and animals
that are most threatened by deforestation. We believe
that a bold new approach, which we call conservation
concessions, provides a potentially powerful way to

expand the green market from its present dependence on products to the broader notion of green services— the opportunity to purchase biodiversity preservation directly.

The feasibility of this strategy relies on economics. Huge tracts of public forest in the developing world are being leased for less than $1 per hectare a year. At those prices, conservation organizations, which have long demonstrated a willingness to pay for the preservation of biodiversity, can afford to outbid competitors for land leases and to compensate local people to manage the intact ecosystems. These agreements are legally and economically no different from logging contracts or any other business deal that grants control over natural resources to a particular group. Indeed, the income that developing countries can generate in this way is equivalent to, and often more stable than, what they could earn through the volatile international markets for timber and agricultural goods.

No Other Choices

One of the greatest advantages of conservation concessions is that they dispel the notion that habitat destruction is inevitable if ecosystems are to generate financial benefits. During a study of cocoa economics in Ghana in the spring of 2000, an official in that country's department of forestry explained to one of our research partners, Eduard Niesten, that Ghana's government cannot be expected to set aside more than the 20 percent of its prized high-canopy forest zone that is already protected by national law. The rest must be used for economic progress, the official said. This pessimistic sentiment is widespread among governments and residents of many developing countries, where economic planning often includes rapid growth of the production of agricultural commodities, especially after logging operations have cleared the land. These activities represent an attractive—and perhaps the only—development option in tropical countries, which tend to have an abundance of land and unskilled labor but insufficient capital to finance more costly endeavors, such as industry.

To examine this issue more closely, we formed a research team with six other investigators at Conservation International's Center for Applied Biodiversity Science in Washington, D.C. Our aim was to study agricultural commodities that are produced in areas designated by ecologists as the world's richest and most threatened in terms of biodiversity. These 25 so-called biodiversity hot spots, which encompass only 1.4 percent of the earth's land surface, have lost at least 70 percent of their primary vegetation. They are also prime habitats for 44 percent of all vascular plant species and 35 percent of all land-dwelling vertebrate species. Based on this three-year study, our team determined that in addition to logging for timber, natural-habitat destruction is rapid and extensive to accommodate the production of five agricultural commodities: beef, soybeans, palm oil, coffee and cocoa.

In the 1980s the expansion of cattle ranches in South America was widely publicized. This activity accounted for 44 percent of deforestation on the continent during that decade. Today one of the greatest threats to South America's tropical biodiversity is the expanding production of soybeans, most of which goes to feed livestock. Since the 1970s soybean cultivation has grown by 13 million hectares in Brazil alone—the fastest expansion of any agricultural product in the tropics known to date. Government subsidies have allowed this activity to move into areas never before touched by agriculture. In neighboring Bolivia, the area devoted to this crop has grown by an average of nearly 35 percent a year since the mid-1960s and is fast approaching one million hectares.

Elsewhere natural forests are being converted at an alarming rate to cultivation of the other three crops in our study. Spread ubiquitously around the world's biodiversity hot spots are coffee and cocoa, occupying 11 and eight million hectares, respectively. Their cultivation has replaced as much as 80 percent of Ivory Coast's original forests. Malaysia leads the production of palm oil, cultivating three million hectares out of the total six million devoted to this commodity globally. Indonesia, which currently grows oil palm on 2.5 million hectares, has vowed to overtake its neighbor as the world's leading producer by planting the 15 million additional hectares that the government has already slated for oil palm plantations.

Certainly the intention of people who convert biologically diverse ecosystems to agriculture or logged forests is to improve their economic lot in life. The sad irony is that these prospects are often unreliable. When countries choose logging and agriculture for lack of better economic options, they often are not competitive in global markets. Indeed, the very nature of export commodity markets is that many producers are not profitable for years at a time because of chronic over-supply. The annual harvest of cocoa and accumulated stocks, for example, exceeded consumption by between 30 and 70 percent each year from 1971 to 1999. Cultivators in West Africa recently resorted to burning their crops in a desperate protest of the situation. Another striking example played out in Bolivia, where in 1996 the imposition of a new tax of $1 per hectare on the country's 22 million hectares of timber concessions resulted in nearly 17 million hectares being abandoned by loggers. In other words, the potential net returns for logging these forests were so low that an additional cost of $1 per hectare per year was enough to make most companies avoid these investments.

No matter the level of economic payoff, all these situations can portend widespread, irreversible loss of biodiversity. The concept of sustainable forestry and farming practices was born of this dilemma—the need to promote economic development while mitigating its probable course of ecological destruction. But our recent studies have convinced us that attempting to give green consumers broader access to agricultural markets is not necessarily a winning option for economic development or conservation in many settings. The share of the global agricultural market that is occupied by green goods is largely limited to those consumers in Europe and the U.S. who have the money for, and an interest in, purchasing such products. This reality effectively eliminates the potential for curtailing deforestation related to many agricultural products—for example, soybeans from Brazil that are eaten by livestock, oil palm in Indonesia that is cultivated for domestic consumption, and trees in Madagascar that are burned locally as fuel [see "The Limits of Buying Green" box].

Even when certified goods—such as coffee, timber and beef—do reach wealthy consumers, the effect is not as significant as some may think. Less than 1 percent of the coffee imported into the U.S. is certified for social or ecological reasons. What is more, most of the land newly devoted to growing coffee beans is for robusta, usually sold in developing countries as instant coffee, rather than arabica, the product sold most commonly in cafés of the industrial world. Green timber fares no better. Even if every board foot of wood imported into the U.S. and Europe from tropical countries were certified, it would make up only 6.5 percent of total production from the tropics. The rest is being sold in regions where consumers have little or no interest in certified timber. Similarly, organically produced beef is

The Limits of Buying Green

A popular strategy for slowing the destruction of tropical forests has been to promote ecologically friendly practices within the agriculture and logging industries. But demand for coffee, timber and other "green" goods that are produced according to these certified practices originates almost entirely in Europe and the U.S., where consumers are willing to pay premium prices to support conservation. These niche markets play an important role in conservation efforts, but they have serious limits.

Unreliable profits restrict the markets for coffee and cocoa. Whether or not they produce green goods, all cultivators of these products must face the uncoordinated nature of global production, which often results in vast oversupply. Cocoa production swelled throughout the 1980s and 1990s, for instance, despite a punishing decline in price. For green consumerism to work in this context, conservationists must find ways not only to make cultivation and harvesting ecologically sound but also to ensure that the products will be profitable in a competitive global market.

A different problem confines the market for green timber. Organizations such as the Mexico-based nonprofit Forest Stewardship Council have certified more than five million hectares of logging activity in Asia, Africa and Latin America. The problem is that almost all the green timber produced in these forests is sold in Europe and the U.S., which together import less than 6.5 percent of the 228 million cubic meters of all timber—green or otherwise—that is produced in the tropics every year. The vast majority of uncertified logging serves the economies outside these regions.

The worse-case scenario occurs when uncertified logging occurs in biodiversity hot spots such as Madagascar, where most of the timber harvested will become charcoal that local people burn for fuel. This island country, which is less than 2 percent the size of neighboring Africa, harbors a staggering diversity of living things that are found nowhere else on the planet, including at least 8,000 species of flowering plant. Madagascar shelters 12 percent of all living primate species, 36 percent of all primate families, and 33 species of lemur that exist virtually nowhere else, making it possibly the world's single most important area for conservation of these animals. And yet because the trees are consumed domestically, wealthy foreign consumers looking to "buy green" have no opportunity to influence the logging of these priceless forest habitats.

A New Green Market

Land set aside for conservation is often deemed an economic asset gone to waste. A new market for green services promises to eliminate this trade-off. International willingness to pay for conservation reflects growing demand for protection of the world's biodiversity, which many developing countries can readily supply. The logic behind this new market is simple: landowners lease natural resources to conservationists, who pay the same as or more than logging companies or other destructive users. These so-called conservation concessions not only protect the land but also finance conservation services and provide employment for local people. A properly executed conservation concession:

Enables host countries to capitalize on their ample supply of biodiversity-rich habitats.

The concession approach alleviates economic reliance on volatile timber and agricultural commodity markets and allows tropical countries to benefit economically by protecting their natural resources. This benefit can be achieved without depreciating the value of the natural resource and without damaging wildlife habitats or other aspects of the environment.

Stimulates economic development by mimicking the payment structure of other business transactions.

Payments cover government taxes and fees, lost employment, and capital investment and are made in hard currency. Part of these fees is directed to the local communities to create jobs and invest in social programs.

Offers immediate, transparent protection for the land in question.

The tangible nature of conservation concessions offers a clear way to quantify the payoff of biodiversity investments. They should also appeal to corporations seeking methods to offset the environmental impacts of their operations with unambiguous benefits.

Catalyzes conservation in situations where creating a national park may be infeasible.

Conservation concessions provide governments with an economically sound motive for creating protected areas that extend beyond park systems. Concession payments also ensure long-term management of these areas, in contrast to many underfunded national parks.

Reduces risk of failure by establishing ongoing economic incentive for cooperation.

Substantial financial risk accompanies business investments in many developing countries, but a well-constructed incentive system based on annual payments in return for resource monitoring and other conservation services should dramatically reduce the temptation to break a concession agreement.

—J.H. and R.R.

growing in popularity in industrial countries. But international trade in beef represents only between 1 and 3 percent of global production; in the developing world, beef production is growing at more than 3 percent a year, primarily to serve domestic markets.

Marketing Green Services

The more we studied the conservation impacts of timber and agricultural commodity markets, the more convinced we became that attempting to support these markets through price premiums for green products is not the only way to encourage conservation. This situation seemed especially tragic when we considered the high demand for biodiversity protection among the international community. A common misperception is that conservation cannot compete directly with most other economic uses of natural resources; in reality, the conservation economy is quite large. The international community—including governments, multilateral development banks and conservation groups—spends at least half a billion dollars annually on biodiversity conservation in the tropics.

This figure is only a small fraction of the global budget that could be directed to biodiversity-rich countries if better investment mechanisms existed. In 1999 an example from Bolivia showed us just how far these financial resources can go. That year Conservation International paid a logging company $100,000 to retire its 45,000-hectare timber concession. As part of the deal, the Bolivian government agreed to integrate the area into adjacent Madidi National Park. Bottom line: an area three times the size of Washington, D.C., received permanent protection for less than the average price of a house in that city.

Working with timber concessions or other lease arrangements enables conservationists to avoid the problems associated with purchasing land outright. Some governments balk at the idea of foreign investors taking permanent control of parts of their territories, especially if they are trying to ensure a renewable stream of revenue from their natural resources. For the same reasons, incorporating land into national parks—as conservationists were able to convince the Bolivian government to do—is also a rare opportunity. That is why the Bolivia experience, and others like it, inspired us to take advantage of the low prices for which millions of hectares of forest could be leased in the tropics.

We developed the conservation concession approach to leasing land with several major goals in mind [see "A New Green Market" box]. Most important, perhaps, was that a portion of the concession payments would be directed to local communities to support employment and social services. In the same way that a logging company would pay local residents wages and benefits to work in the mills, the financier of the conservation concession would hire them to preserve the forest.

Once we had developed a clear set of criteria for this newfangled green services market, we set off to create a series of pilot conservation concessions.

Partnering with Parks

National parks are an important component of any nation's conservation plan. In countries such as Guatemala and Indonesia, conservation concessions can extend the protection that parks offer, especially in areas that allow economic activities such as logging.

GUATEMALA

Conservation Context: In 1990 the government of Guatemala created the two-million-hectare Maya Biosphere Reserve (MBR). The reserve includes a multiple-use area where commercial exploitation of forest resources is allowed, but its core zones are protected against all activities other than those judged to be environmentally benign, such as scientific research and ecotourism.

What's at Stake: The MBR is the largest remaining tropical forest in Guatemala, and it constitutes a major part of a Mesoamerican biological corridor that shelters the jaguar and other species with extensive ranges.

The Threat: Commercial logging (especially for mahogany) and agricultural invasion threaten forests in the multiple-use zone.

Proposed Concession: Later this year Conservation International and its Guatemalan partner, ProPetén, hope to finalize conservation-concession contracts with the communities that manage some 75,000 hectares of forest within the multiple-use zone. These additional conservation areas will begin to provide habitat links between the reserve's core zones of Tikal and El Mirador national parks.

INDONESIA

Conservation Context: Siberut National Park protects just under half of the 400,000-hectare island of Siberut, off the western coast of Sumatra. Only about 60 percent of the 205,000 hectares outside the park remain naturally forested.

What's at Stake: Three distinct types of forest habitat, including lowland tropical rain forest and freshwater swamp, support a diversity of life. Four of the island's primate species—Kloss gibbon, pig-tailed langur, Mentawai langur and Mentawai macaque—live nowhere else in the world. About 35,000 Mentawaian people, who maintain a Neolithic social structure, also rely heavily on the island's forest resources for their subsistence.

The Threat: Pending concessions for commercial logging and oil palm plantations threaten 80 percent of the island—including areas within the park.

Proposed Concession: The local government of Siberut and Conservation International are negotiating a conservation concession that could extend the area protected by the park and curtail encroachment by logging and agriculture.

—J.R. and R.R.

Among the first countries we visited, early in 2000, was Peru. There we planned to compete for part of the 800,000 hectares of Amazon forest that the government was putting up for lease in an international auction. What transpired during our negotiations confirmed our theory that the economic value of forest resources in Peru—and many other regions of the world—is poor at best. Indeed, the auction began with a proposed minimum bid of between $1 and $4 per hectare a year and involved forestry companies from Europe and North and South America in addition to us. In a matter of months, however, the auction was called off because the other potential bidders lost interest in these concessions, presumably because the base price was too high. The fate of that particular forest remains to be determined, but we had planted a seed that took root in the fertile ground prepared by the Peruvian conservation community.

Peru had been undergoing the final revisions of its forest and wildlife law, a process in which several conservation groups were seeking alternatives to logging leases for Peru's forests. In April 2001 the government chose to include conservation concessions as a legal use of its 67 million hectares of public forest. We had entered the original bidding arena without knowing for certain that we would be allowed to compete, so this was good news. At around that time, a Peruvian conservation group, the Amazon Conservation Association, approached us. The group's members wanted to use a conservation concession to secure critical natural habitat where they were setting up an ecological research station. Under the new Peruvian law, concessions could be acquired by applying for specific areas of interest to the bidder. We leaped at the chance to help launch Peru's first conservation concession.

Thanks to the scientific and community work of the Amazon Conservation Association, legal advice from the Peruvian Environmental Law Society (SPDA), assistance from independent environmental consultant Enrique Toledo, and the enthusiastic support of Peru's Minister of Agriculture, Carlos Amat y Leon, Peru established the Los Amigos conservation concession in July 2001. The agreement centered on a renewable 40-year lease for the conservation management and study of 130,000 hectares of tropical forest. This land forms part of an ecological corridor that links Manu and Bahuaja-Sonene national parks in Peru and protects many of that country's 25,000 species of flora and 1,700 species of birds.

Catching On

Over the course of our Los Amigos negotiations, we also conducted discussions for pilot projects in Guyana and Guatemala. In September 2000 the government of Guyana issued to Conservation International an exploratory permit for a conservation concession of approximately 80,000 hectares in the southern part of the country. During the subsequent months, we have worked with forest commission officials to negotiate the terms of a renewable 25-year contract. We hope to conclude the deal for this uninhabited area of forest later this year.

In Guatemala the national government had already issued timber concessions within the country's two-million-hectare Maya Biosphere Reserve to local communities. These people, who live within the reserve's multiple-use zone, where logging and other economic activities are permitted, are currently producing certified green timber from their forests. Two communities, however, have proposed to forgo logging and instead lease standing trees—and the obligation to protect the ecosystem in which they reside—to conservationists. The communities, together representing about 110 households, could use their new revenue stream from the proposed concession deal to pay salaries for conservation managers, to invest in projects such as guiding tourists to nearby archaeological sites, and to provide community social services such as education and health care. The proposed concessions, which would preserve both pristine forest and a wealth of Mayan ruins, span approximately 75,000 hectares bordering a national park [see "Partnering with Parks" box]. The Guatemala and Guyana deals, both developed and financed by Conservation International's Center for Applied Biodiversity Science and the Global Conservation Fund, represent two very different settings for concessions.

At many turns in our negotiations over the past two years, we have faced scrutiny and skepticism about conservation concessions, from governments and conservationists alike. But the bold actions that some governments, together with significant financial supporters, have taken to adopt this approach indicate that it is viable both as an economic alternative and as a conservation tool.

And the idea is catching on. Last year we received a phone call from a man in Ecuador who had traveled six hours to the nearest international phone line so he could ask about establishing a conservation concession in his coastal forest community. Halfway around the world we struck up a partnership with a small non-governmental organization in Indonesia that is keen to experiment with this concept as a way to protect that nation's fragile marine ecosystems.

Now, along with other colleagues, we are looking at the feasibility of conservation concessions across Africa, Asia and Latin America, and we predict that this approach will transfer readily to many areas. If we are right, conservation concessions may indeed be able to bring to life a global market for green services.

More to Explore

Can Sustainable Management Save Tropical Forests?
Richard E. Rice, Raymond E. Gullison and John W. Reid in *Scientific American*, Vol. 276, No. 4, pages 44–49; April 1997.
Biodiversity Hotspots for Conservation Priorities.
Norman Myers, Russell A. Mittermeier, Cristina G. Mittermeier, Gustavo A. B. da Fonseca

and Jennifer Kent in *Nature*, Vol. 403, pages
853–858; February 24, 2000.
**Effectiveness of Parks in Protecting Tropical
Biodiversity.** Aaron G. Bruner, Raymond E.
Gullison, Richard E. Rice and Gustavo A. B. da
Fonseca in *Science*, Vol. 291, pages 125–128;
January 5, 2001.

About the Authors

JARED HARDNER and *RICHARD RICE* have
collaborated on economic studies of biodiversity
conservation in South America, Africa and Asia for
the past 10 years. Hardner earned a master's degree in
natural resource economics from Yale University in
1996, and four years later he co-founded Hardner &
Gullison Associates, an environmental consulting firm
based in Palo Alto, Calif. Rice received both a master's
degree in economics and a doctorate in natural resources
from the University of Michigan in 1983. In 1992 he
joined Conservation International (CI), and in 1999 he
accepted his current position as chief economist of the
organization's Center for Applied Biodiversity Science
in Washington, D.C., where Hardner also serves as a
research fellow. The authors would like to express
their thanks to collaborators Anita Akella, Gregory
Dicum, Philip Fearnside, Sharon Flynn, Ted Gullison,
Chris LaFranchi, Michelle Manion, Shelley Ratay, the
staff of CI's offices in Guyana and Peru, and the staff
of ProPetén in Guatemala.

"The Unmet Need for
4. Family Planning"

By Malcolm Potts

Women and men in many countries still lack adequate access to contraceptives. Unless they are given the option of controlling their fertility, severe environmental and health problems loom in the coming century throughout large parts of the world.

During 1999, the world's population surged past the six-billion mark. The most recent billion was added in just 12 years. Such numerical milestones, like this month's calendrical rollover, are of course just arbitrary artifacts of our decimal counting system, yet they offer a suitable occasion for taking stock of important trends.

Worldwide, the average number of children born to each woman—the fertility rate—has declined over the past three decades, from almost six to 2.9, prompting some commentators to venture that overpopulation may no longer be a threat.

They are mistaken. Global population is still increasing by about 78 million people—a number equivalent to a new Germany—each year. Moreover, because large families were common in most of the world until recently, many countries have very large numbers of young people.

This population structure means that rapid growth is sure to continue for decades to come, almost all of it in developing countries, where family-planning services may be inadequate or nonexistent. In nations that lack adequate medical, financial and educational institutions, not to mention food and water supplies, the result of a fast-growing population is much human misery. The quality of life of a large proportion of humanity during the coming century—and the future size of the global population—will depend critically on how quickly the world can satisfy the currently unmet demand for family planning.

Every day more than 400,000 conceptions take place around the world. About a quarter to half are deliberate, happy decisions, but half are unintended, and many of these are bitterly regretted. A series of surveys in over 50 low-income countries has asked more than 300,000 women how many children they want to have. In nearly every country surveyed, women are bearing more offspring than they intend. When I practiced obstetrics in a London hospital in the 1960s, I would ask new mothers, "When do you want your next baby?" Many replied, "Doctor, I was just going to ask you about that." They were glad, in other words, that I had opened the door on to an embarrassing but important topic. My boss in the hospital, however, berated me for discussing birth control. I learned that family planning was wanted but controversial.

During the past 30 years, many countries have greatly improved their provision of family-planning services. Contraceptive use in the developing world has risen from one in 10 couples to more than half of all couples. A 15 percent increase in the use of contraceptives means, on average, about one fewer birth per woman. Thus, in Ethiopia only 4 percent of women use contraception and the fertility rate is seven, while in South Africa 53 percent use some method, and average fertility is 3.3. The desire for smaller families is spreading. In 1998 researchers associated with the Asian Development Bank in Laos, one of the world's poorest countries, invited people there to say what help they wanted most. The men requested jobs, but the women's number-one priority was family planning.

The unmet need for contraceptives is clearly on a different scale in Ethiopia or West Africa, where women commonly bear six children, than in, say, Italy, which has one of the lowest fertility rates in the world—1.2. Yet wherever people have said they want fewer children and family planning has been made available, fertility has fallen. What they need is access to a variety of methods, backed up by safe abortion if they choose it. The pill, the condom and injectables are the types most likely to be widely useful in developing countries.

Obstacles to Progress

The trouble is that in some parts of the world contraceptives are either too expensive or simply unavailable to the people who most need them. The female condom, a recent development, may prove too costly for use in the most impoverished regions. I have seen women in Sri Lanka who were eager to control their fertility but so poor that they had to buy oral contraceptive tablets five at a time rather than in a monthly pack of 21. An estimated 120 million couples in developing countries do not want another child soon but have no access to family-planning methods or have inadequate information on the topic. Consequently, pregnancy too often brings despair instead of joy.

Limiting family size can be difficult. A healthy woman may be fertile between the ages of 12 to 50, and men produce viable sperm from puberty until death. Many couples engage in intercourse without taking precautions because they cannot find or afford contraception. For others, sex can be a violent act that leaves a woman with no opportunity to protect herself against unwanted pregnancy. A survey conducted in 1998 in the Indian state of Uttar Pradesh found that 43 percent of wives had been beaten by their husbands. If such women are to be helped, contraceptives have to be very easy to get.

In many countries, laws create hurdles. Japanese women were until this past year forbidden access to the pill and so had to rely heavily on abortion. Until the early 1990s, condom sales in Ireland were restricted to certain outlets, and even today some pharmacists refuse to sell them. The Indian government does not allow injectable contraceptives to be used, although the method has proved popular in neighboring Bangladesh. The rich typically have ways to get around such obstacles, but the poor do not.

In some nations, contraceptives are available only by medical prescription. This means that they cannot reach the many villages in Asia and Africa where there are few or no doctors. In Thailand, large numbers of women started to use birth-control pills as soon as nurses and midwives were given the authority to distribute them. Restrictive medical practices limit family-planning choices and make contraception more expensive but add nothing to safety. Birth-control pills are safer than aspirin. The world would be a healthier place if oral contraceptives were available in every corner store and cigarettes were limited to prescription use.

Changes in South Korea and the Philippines present a stark example of how family size plummets when consumers are offered a range of appropriately priced contraceptive options through convenient channels. In 1960 families in both countries had an average of about six children. By 1998 fertility had fallen to 1.7 in South Korea. In the Philippines, though, fertility was still 3.7, because family-planning help is harder to get there. Economic research strongly suggests that small family size is a prerequisite to higher per capita income. The difference in fertility rates between South Korea and the Philippines thus probably goes a long way toward explaining why income in South Korea reached $10,550 per person in 1998, while in the Philippines it was only $1,200.

In Colombia, fertility fell from six to 3.5 in only 15 years after contraceptives became widely available in 1968. In Thailand the same jump took a mere eight years. That identical transition took the U.S. almost 60 years, from 1842 to 1900: antivice activist Anthony Comstock persuaded Congress to outlaw contraceptives in 1873, and it was not until 1965 that the Supreme Court struck down the last laws banning contraception. No surveys of desired family size were conducted in the U.S. in the 19th century, but I suspect that many couples had more children than they intended.

The contrasting cases of Bangladesh and Pakistan illustrate particularly well how family planning can help women escape centuries of obedience to their mothers-in-law and of subservience to their husbands. Until a civil war in 1971, these two countries were a single political unit, and women had an average of seven births. Over the past 20 years, Bangladesh has made a systematic effort to provide a variety of fertility regulation methods, including the pill and injectables. With these, women can control whether or not they become pregnant—an advantage they may lack if they rely on their husband's use of a condom. As a consequence, in spite of appalling poverty, fertility has fallen to 3.3 as contraceptive use among Bangladeshi women has risen from 5 percent in the 1970s to 42 percent today. Similar changes have not occurred in Pakistan, where most of the population still does not have access to fertility regulation, and women there bear an average of 5.3 children. These differences will have consequences that will last well into the 21st century. Although Bangladesh will increase its numbers by 65 percent by 2050, Pakistan will probably by then have reached 2.2 times as many people as it has today.

Offering Choices

My lifetime has seen the most far-reaching demographic changes in history. Global population has almost tripled since I was born in 1935; it has quadrupled during the past century. The primary reason is a welcome decline in infant and child mortality brought about by the spread of public health measures such as vaccination. Unfortunately, this progress has not been accompanied by a parallel spread of modern contraception.

It is only since the 19th century that families have routinely seen more than two children survive to the next generation—otherwise there would have been a population explosion centuries ago. Large families are a recent, and temporary, anomaly. Small families reduce stress on the environment, benefit economies—and gain directly themselves. Research in Thailand has shown that children born into families with two or fewer off-spring are more likely to enter and stay in school than are children from larger families of four or more youngsters. When pregnancies are spaced at least two years apart, both mother and baby are significantly more likely to survive. Worldwide, one woman dies every minute as a consequence of pregnancy, childbirth or abortion. Some 99 percent of these deaths are in developing countries.

Better access to contraception would reduce this toll substantially by saving on the order of 100,000 women's lives a year.

When Paul Ehrlich wrote his well-known book *The Population Bomb* in 1968, Western governments were just beginning to support family planning in countries such as South Korea. At the time, demographers and politicians spoke about "population control," giving the impression that rich countries were telling others how their people should live. Today we know that the surest way to bring down the birth rate is to listen to what people are asking for and to offer them a range of choices. Adults are capable of making up their own minds about what they want.

Many people in the developing world can afford a small payment for modern contraceptives, but poor countries cannot meet the full cost of manufacturing, distributing and promoting them. A few governments, such as those of India and Indonesia, provide contraception free or at subsidized prices. Yet many nations are too impoverished or too corrupt to make family planning a priority. For many of the 1.3 billion people around the world who live on a dollar a day or less, donations from rich countries are essential—and wanted.

This consensus achieved public prominence in 1994, when the United Nations organized the International Conference on Population and Development in Cairo. The program agreed to at Cairo broadened the traditional scope of population activities to include not only family planning but also efforts to reduce maternal mortality, to treat sexually transmitted infections and to slow the spread of AIDS. The price tag foreseen for the year 2000 was $17 billion, of which $6.5 billion (in 1998 dollars) was to come from developed nations.

Will that money be available? Not on present showing. In 1998 the total flow of foreign aid from rich to poor countries was the lowest in 30 years. Of this amount, only about 2 percent was allocated to assist family planning and reproductive health. Indeed, the U.S. has cut its funding for international family-planning programs over the past few years.

Developed countries last year provided only one third of the money they had pledged to give at Cairo. Because of the shortfall, even meeting the growing cost of contraceptives and of antibiotics to treat sexually transmitted diseases will be difficult in some places.

Counting the Unborn

Many of the parents of the 21st century's children are already born, so credible estimates of the future world population can be made to about 2050. The latest projections from the U.N. Population Division, issued in 1998, envisage a global total between 7.3 billion and 10.7 billion in 2050, with 8.9 billion considered the most likely figure.

It is crucial to realize, however, that this "most likely" number assumes a continuing rise in the rate of use of contraceptives and consequent widespread decline in birth rates. Specifically, it supposes that fertility in developing countries will reach 2.1 by 2050. With current trends, this actually seems unlikely. Large regions of Africa and southern Asia have fertilities far above 2.1, and unless more funds for family planning become available, I see no reason to think fertility will fall as much as the U.N.'s "most likely" figure assumes.

The 1998 projections necessarily take account of the relentless spread of the AIDS virus in many countries. It now seems probable that between 30 million and 40 million people will be infected by 2010—more than the number of combatants and civilians killed in World War II. AIDS has lowered average life expectancy by seven years in the 29 most affected African countries. Yet despite this devastating impact, the population of Africa is set to grow from 750 million today to more than 1.7 billion in 2050 because of the momentum built into the population's youth-heavy age structure.

Population projections are not predictions but "what if" statements. If support for family planning remains inadequate, three possibilities, not mutually exclusive, suggest themselves.

First, birth rates could remain higher than the U.N. assumes they will in its projections. Small variations in the rate at which fertility declines in the next few decades will have profound consequences well into the 22nd century. For example, if Nigeria, now at a population of 114 million, were to achieve a replacement-level fertility of 2.1 in 2010, its population would stabilize at 290 million in about 2100. If the country did not reach 2.1 children for each woman until 2030, the population would rise to 450 million, corresponding to a population density 40 percent greater than that of the Netherlands today. If replacement-level fertility does not arrive until 2050, Nigeria's population could theoretically reach 700 million. In fact, disease or starvation would limit population in a most inhumane way long before then.

The second possible outcome of a failure to expand family planning is that some governments might be tempted to impose strict population-control measures such as those adopted by China. In the 1950s and 1960s Mao Tse-tung encouraged large families for ideological reasons. (The Taiwanese, who had excellent access to contraceptives, had one of the quickest fertility declines in history.) By the time the Chinese woke up to the need to slow their growth in 1979, the momentum was so great that the state felt compelled to limit couples to just one child. Even with this policy, the number of Chinese grew from 989 million in 1979 to 1.25 billion today—a gain only slightly less than the total population of the U.S., in a country of roughly the same size.

A third possibility is that abortion rates may rise. Each woman around the world now averages one induced abortion in her lifetime. A recent calculation based on African data suggests that if contraceptives are not available to meet the growing demand, a sixfold jump in abortions will be necessary for birth rates to fall in line with the U.N. assumptions. That sort of jump would kill thousands of women, because abortions are often performed unsafely.

The success or failure of national family-planning efforts in the opening years of the coming millennium will divide the world along a new geopolitical fault line. Those newly industrialized nations of Asia and Latin America that see family size settle at two or fewer children by about 2010 will join the club of rich Western nations. They will have a slowly aging population, and the number of their citizens older than 60 will double by 2050.

The other set of countries, in Africa and the Indian subcontinent, will be overwhelmed by burgeoning population growth. Vast cohorts of young people will grow up with little education and even fewer job opportunities. Some may form politically unstable gangs in exploding city slums; others may try to eke out a living by cutting down the remaining forests.

The Cairo conference recognized "the crucial contribution that early stabilization of the world population would make towards the achievement of sustainable development." Transforming the global economy to a biologically sustainable one may well prove the greatest challenge humanity faces. Ultimately, we have to construct a world in which we take no more from the environment than it can replace and put out no more pollution than it can absorb.

If this transition is to succeed, societies will have to reduce both levels of consumption and population sizes. Even today it would be impossible for the planet to sustain a Western standard of living for everyone.

Many experts predict that a billion people will be facing severe water shortages by 2025.

Fortunately, much expertise has accumulated about how to make family planning available. The cost to developed countries of meeting this vital need is less than $5 per person per year. That amount is trivial in comparison with the financial, environmental and human costs of inaction.

Further Information

Seeking Common Ground: Demographic Goals and Individual Choice. Steven Sinding, with John Ross and Allan Rosenfield. Population Reference Bureau, Washington, D.C., May 1994.

Hopes and Realities: Closing the Gap between Women's Aspirations and Their Reproductive Experiences. Alan Guttmacher Institute, New York, 1995.

Sex and the Birth Rate: Human Biology, Demographic Change, and Access to Fertility-Regulation Methods. Malcolm Potts in *Population and Development Review*, Vol. 23, No. 1, pages 1–39; March 1997.

6 Billion: A Time for Choices. The State of World Population 1999. UNFPA, United Nations Population Fund, New York, 1999. Available at **www.unfpa.org/swp/swpmain.htm** on the World Wide Web.

Let Every Child Be Wanted: How Social Marketing Is Revolutionizing Contraceptive Use around the World. Philip D. Harvey. Greenwood Publishing, 1999.

About the Author

MALCOLM POTTS is a British physician who also holds a doctorate in embryology, which he earned at the University of Cambridge. For the past 30 years, he has worked with a variety of groups in the design and implementation of family-planning services and in AIDS prevention. He is a board member of Population Services International, among other organizations, and the author or co-author of several books on aspects of human fertility. Last year Potts published *Ever Since Adam and Eve: The Evolution of Human Sexuality*. He is Bixby Professor in the School of Public Health at the University of California, Berkeley.

"Is Global Warming
5. Harmful to Health?"

By Paul R. Epstein

Computer models indicate that many diseases will surge as the earth's atmosphere heats up. Signs of the predicted troubles have begun to appear.

T oday few scientists doubt the atmosphere is warming. Most also agree that the rate of heating is accelerating and that the consequences of this temperature change could become increasingly disruptive. Even high school students can reel off some projected outcomes: the oceans will warm, and glaciers will melt, causing sea levels to rise and salt water to inundate settlements along many low-lying coasts. Meanwhile the regions suitable for farming will shift. Weather patterns should also become more erratic and storms more severe.

Yet less familiar effects could be equally detrimental. Notably, computer models predict that global warming, and other climate alterations it induces, will expand the incidence and distribution of many serious medical disorders. Disturbingly, these forecasts seem to be coming true.

Heating of the atmosphere can influence health through several routes. Most directly, it can generate more, stronger and hotter heat waves, which will become especially treacherous if the evenings fail to bring cooling relief. Unfortunately, a lack of nighttime cooling seems to be in the cards; the atmosphere is heating unevenly and is showing the biggest rises at night, in winter and at latitudes higher than about 50 degrees. In some places, the number of deaths related to heat waves is projected to double by 2020. Prolonged heat can, moreover, enhance production of smog and the dispersal of allergens. Both effects have been linked to respiratory symptoms.

Global warming can also threaten human well-being profoundly, if somewhat less directly, by revising weather patterns—particularly by pumping up the frequency and intensity of floods and droughts and by causing rapid swings in the weather. As the atmosphere has warmed over the past century, droughts in arid areas have persisted longer, and massive bursts of precipitation have become more common. Aside from causing death by drowning or starvation, these disasters promote by various means the emergence, resurgence and spread of infectious disease.

That prospect is deeply troubling, because infectious illness is a genie that can be very hard to put back into its bottle. It may kill fewer people in one fell swoop than a raging flood or an extended drought, but once it takes root in a community, it often defies eradication and can invade other areas.

The control issue looms largest in the developing world, where resources for prevention and treatment can be scarce. But the technologically advanced nations, too, can fall victim to surprise attacks—as happened last year when the West Nile virus broke out for the first time in North America, killing seven New Yorkers. In these days of international commerce and travel, an infectious disorder that appears in one part of the world can quickly become a problem continents away if the disease-causing agent, or pathogen, finds itself in a hospitable environment.

Floods and droughts associated with global climate change could undermine health in other ways as well. They could damage crops and make them vulnerable to infection and infestations by pests and choking weeds, thereby reducing food supplies and potentially contributing to malnutrition. And they could permanently or semipermanently displace entire populations in developing countries, leading to overcrowding and the diseases connected with it, such as tuberculosis.

Weather becomes more extreme and variable with atmospheric heating in part because the warming accelerates the water cycle: the process in which water vapor, mainly from the oceans, rises into the atmosphere before condensing out as precipitation. A warmed atmosphere heats the oceans (leading to faster evaporation), and it holds more moisture than a cool one. When the extra water condenses, it more frequently drops from the sky as larger downpours. While the oceans are being heated, so is the land, which can become highly parched in dry areas. Parching enlarges the pressure gradients that cause winds to develop, leading to turbulent winds, tornadoes and other powerful storms. In addition, the altered pressure and temperature gradients that accompany global warming can shift the distribution of when and where storms, floods and droughts occur.

I will address the worrisome health effects of global warming and disrupted climate patterns in greater detail, but I should note that the consequences may not all be bad. Very high temperatures in hot regions may reduce snail populations, which have a role in transmitting schistosomiasis, a parasitic disease. High winds may at times disperse pollution. Hotter winters in normally chilly areas may reduce cold-related heart attacks and respiratory ailments. Yet overall, the undesirable effects of more variable weather are likely to include new stresses and nasty surprises that will overshadow any benefits.

Mosquitoes Rule in the Heat

Diseases relayed by mosquitoes—such as malaria, dengue fever, yellow fever and several kinds of encephalitis— are among those eliciting the greatest concern as the world warms. Mosquitoes acquire disease-causing microorganisms when they take a blood meal from an infected animal or person. Then the pathogen reproduces inside the insects, which may deliver disease-causing doses to the next individuals they bite.

Mosquito-borne disorders are projected to become increasingly prevalent because their insect carriers, or "vectors," are very sensitive to meteorological conditions. Cold can be a friend to humans, because it limits mosquitoes to seasons and regions where temperatures stay above certain minimums. Winter freezing kills many eggs, larvae and adults outright. *Anopheles* mosquitoes, which transmit malaria parasites (such as *Plasmodium falciparum*), cause sustained outbreaks of malaria only where temperatures routinely exceed 60 degrees Fahrenheit. Similarly, *Aedes aegypti* mosquitoes, responsible for yellow fever and dengue fever, convey virus only where temperatures rarely fall below 50 degrees F.

Excessive heat kills insects as effectively as cold does. Nevertheless, within their survivable range of temperatures, mosquitoes proliferate faster and bite more as the air becomes warmer. At the same time, greater heat speeds the rate at which pathogens inside them reproduce and mature. At 68 degrees F, the immature *P. falciparum* parasite takes 26 days to develop fully, but at 77 degrees F, it takes only 13 days. The *Anopheles* mosquitoes that spread this malaria parasite live only several weeks; warmer temperatures raise the odds that the parasites will mature in time for the mosquitoes to transfer the infection. As whole areas heat up, then, mosquitoes could expand into formerly forbidden territories, bringing illness with them. Further, warmer nighttime and winter temperatures may enable them to cause more disease for longer periods in the areas they already inhabit.

The extra heat is not alone in encouraging a rise in mosquito-borne infections. Intensifying floods and droughts resulting from global warming can each help trigger outbreaks by creating breeding grounds for insects whose dessicated eggs remain viable and hatch in still water. As floods recede, they leave puddles. In times of drought, streams can become stagnant pools, and people may put out containers to catch water; these pools and pots, too, can become incubators for new mosquitoes. And the insects can gain another boost if climate change or other processes (such as alterations of habitats by humans) reduce the populations of predators that normally keep mosquitoes in check.

Mosquitoes on the March

Malaria and dengue fever are two of the mosquito-borne diseases most likely to spread dramatically as global temperatures head upward. Malaria (marked by chills, fever, aches and anemia) already kills 3,000 people, mostly children, every day. Some models project that by the end of the 21st century, ongoing warming will have enlarged the zone of potential malaria transmission from an area containing 45 percent of the world's population to an area containing about 60 percent. That news is bad indeed, considering that no vaccine is available and that the causative parasites are becoming resistant to standard drugs.

True to the models, malaria is reappearing north and south of the tropics. The U.S. has long been home to *Anopheles* mosquitoes, and malaria circulated here decades ago. By the 1980s mosquito-control programs and other public health measures had restricted the disorder to California. Since 1990, however, when the hottest decade on record began, outbreaks of locally transmitted malaria have occurred during hot spells in Texas, Florida, Georgia, Michigan, New Jersey and New York (as well as in Toronto). These episodes undoubtedly started with a traveler or stowaway mosquito carrying malaria parasites. But the parasites clearly found friendly conditions in the U.S.—enough warmth and humidity, and plenty of mosquitoes able to transport them to victims who had not traveled. Malaria has returned to the Korean peninsula, parts of southern Europe and the former Soviet Union and to the coast of South Africa along the Indian Ocean.

Dengue, or "breakbone," fever (a severe flulike viral illness that sometimes causes fatal internal bleeding) is spreading as well. Today it afflicts an estimated 50 million to 100 million in the tropics and subtropics (mainly in urban areas and their surroundings). It has broadened its range in the Americas over the past 10 years and had reached down to Buenos Aires by the end of the 1990s. It has also found its way to northern Australia. Neither a vaccine nor a specific drug treatment is yet available.

Although these expansions of malaria and dengue fever certainly fit the predictions, the cause of that growth cannot be traced conclusively to global warming. Other factors could have been involved as well—for instance, disruption of the environment in ways that favor mosquito proliferation, declines in mosquito-control and other public health programs, and rises in

Changes Are Already Underway

Computer models have predicted that global warming would produce several changes in the highlands: summit glaciers (like North Polar sea ice) would begin to melt, and plants, mosquitoes and mosquito-borne diseases would migrate upward into regions formerly too cold for them (*diagram*). All these predictions are coming true. This convergence strongly suggests that the upward expansion of mosquitoes and mosquito-borne diseases documented in the past 15 years (*list at bottom*) has stemmed, at least in part, from rising temperatures.

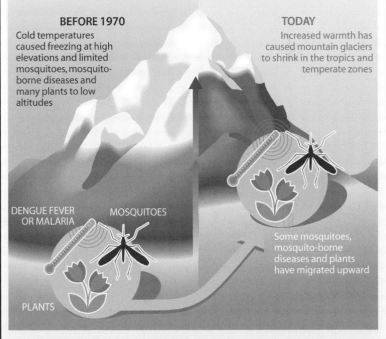

BEFORE 1970
Cold temperatures caused freezing at high elevations and limited mosquitoes, mosquito-borne diseases and many plants to low altitudes

TODAY
Increased warmth has caused mountain glaciers to shrink in the tropics and temperate zones

DENGUE FEVER OR MALARIA

MOSQUITOES

Some mosquitoes, mosquito-borne diseases and plants have migrated upward

PLANTS

WHERE DISEASES OR THEIR CARRIERS HAVE REACHED HIGHER ELEVATIONS

Malaria
Highlands of Ethiopia, Rwanda, Uganda and Zimbabwe
Usamabara Mountains, Tanzania
Highlands of Papua New Guinea and West Papua (Irian Jaya)

Dengue fever
San Jose, Costa Rica
Taxco, Mexico

Aedes aegypti **mosquitoes**
(can spread dengue fever and yellow fever)
Eastern Andes Mountains, Colombia
Northern highlands of India

drug and pesticide resistance. The case for a climatic contribution becomes stronger, however, when other projected consequences of global warming appear in concert with disease outbreaks.

Such is the case in highlands around the world. There, as anticipated, warmth is climbing up many mountains, along with plants and butterflies, and summit glaciers are melting. Since 1970 the elevation at which temperatures are always below freezing has ascended almost 500 feet in the tropics. Marching upward, too, are mosquitoes and mosquito-borne diseases.

In the 19th century, European colonists in Africa settled in the cooler mountains to escape the dangerous swamp air (*"mal aria"*) that fostered disease in the low-lands. Today many of those havens are compromised. Insects and insect-borne infections are being reported at high elevations in South and Central America, Asia, and east and central Africa. Since 1980 *Ae. aegypti* mosquitoes, once limited by temperature thresholds to low altitudes, have been found above one mile in the highlands of northern India and at 1.3 miles in the Colombian Andes. Their presence magnifies the risk that dengue and yellow fever may follow. Dengue fever itself has struck at the mile mark in Taxco, Mexico. Patterns of insect migration change faster in the mountains than they do at sea level. Those alterations can thus serve as indicators of climate change and of diseases likely to expand their range.

Opportunists Like
Sequential Extremes

The increased climate variability accompanying warming will probably be more important than the rising heat itself in fueling unwelcome outbreaks of certain vector-borne illnesses. For instance, warm winters followed by hot, dry summers (a pattern that could become all too familiar as the atmosphere heats up) favor the transmission of St. Louis encephalitis and other infections that cycle among birds, urban mosquitoes and humans.

This sequence seems to have abetted the surprise emergence of the West Nile virus in New York City last year. No one knows how this virus found its way into the U.S. But one reasonable explanation for its persistence and amplification here centers on the weather's effects on *Culex pipiens* mosquitoes, which accounted for the bulk of the transmission. These urban dwellers typically lay their eggs in damp basements, gutters, sewers and polluted pools of water.

The interaction between the weather, the mosquitoes and the virus probably went something like this: The mild winter of 1998–99 enabled many of the mosquitoes to survive into the spring, which arrived early. Drought in spring and summer concentrated nourishing organic matter in their breeding areas and simultaneously killed off mosquito predators, such as lacewings and lady-bugs, that would otherwise have helped limit mosquito populations. Drought would also have led birds to congregate more, as they shared fewer and smaller watering holes, many of which were frequented, naturally, by mosquitoes.

Once mosquitoes acquired the virus, the heat wave that accompanied the drought would speed up viral maturation inside the insects. Consequently, as infected mosquitoes sought blood meals, they could spread the virus to birds at a rapid clip. As bird after bird became infected, so did more mosquitoes, which ultimately fanned out to infect human beings. Torrential rains toward the end of August provided new puddles for the breeding of C. *pipiens* and other mosquitoes, unleashing an added crop of potential virus carriers.

Like mosquitoes, other disease-conveying vectors tend to be "pests"—opportunists that reproduce quickly and thrive under disturbed conditions unfavorable to species with more specialized needs. In the 1990s climate variability contributed to the appearance in humans of a new rodent-borne ailment: the hantavirus pulmonary syndrome, a highly lethal infection of the lungs. This infection can jump from animals to humans when people inhale viral particles hiding in the secretions and excretions of rodents. The sequential weather extremes that set the stage for the first human eruption, in the U.S. Southwest in 1993, were long-lasting drought interrupted by intense rains.

First, a regional drought helped to reduce the pool of animals that prey on rodents—raptors (owls, eagles, prairie falcons, red-tailed hawks and kestrels), coyotes

El Niño's Message

Scientists often gain insight into the workings of complicated systems by studying subsystems. In that spirit, investigators concerned about global warming's health effects are assessing outcomes of the El Niño/ Southern Oscillation (ENSO), a climate process that produces many of the same meteorological changes predicted for a warming world. The findings are not reassuring.

"El Niño" refers to an oceanic phenomenon that materializes every five years or so in the tropical Pacific. The ocean off Peru becomes unusually warm and stays that way for months before returning to normal or going to a cold extreme (La Niña). The name "Southern Oscillation" refers to atmospheric changes that happen in tandem with the Pacific's shifts to warmer or cooler conditions.

During an El Niño, evaporation from the heated eastern Pacific can lead to abnormally heavy rains in parts of South America and Africa; meanwhile other areas of South America and Africa and parts of Southeast Asia and Australia suffer droughts. Atmospheric pressure changes over the tropical Pacific also have ripple effects throughout the globe, generally yielding milder winters in some northern regions of the U.S. and western Canada. During a La Niña, weather patterns in the affected areas may go to opposite extremes.

The incidence of vector-borne and waterborne diseases climbs during El Niño and La Niña years, especially in areas hit by floods or droughts. Long-term studies in Colombia, Venezuela, India and Pakistan reveal, for instance, that malaria surges in the wake of El Niños. And my colleagues and I at Harvard University have shown that regions stricken by flooding or drought during the El Niño of 1997–98 (the strongest of the century) often had to contend as well with a convergence of diseases borne by mosquitoes, rodents and water. Additionally, in many dry areas, fires raged out of control, polluting the air for miles around.

ENSO is not merely a warning of troubles to come; it is likely to be an engine for those troubles. Several climate models predict that as the atmosphere and oceans heat up, El Niños themselves will become more common and severe—which means that the weather disasters they produce and the diseases they promote could become more prevalent as well.

Indeed, the ENSO pattern has already begun to change. Since 1976 the intensity, duration and pace of El Niños have increased. And during the 1990s, every year was marked by an El Niño or La Niña extreme. Those trends bode ill for human health in the 21st century.

—P.R.E.

and snakes. Then, as drought yielded to unusually heavy rains early in 1993, the rodents found a bounty of food, in the form of grasshoppers and piñon nuts. The resulting population explosion enabled a virus that had been either inactive or isolated in a small group to take hold in many rodents. When drought returned in summer, the animals sought food in human dwellings and brought the disease to people. By fall 1993, rodent numbers had fallen, and the outbreak abated.

Subsequent episodes of hantavirus pulmonary syndrome in the U.S. have been limited, in part because early-warning systems now indicate when rodent-control efforts have to be stepped up and because people have learned to be more careful about avoiding the animals' droppings. But the disease has appeared in Latin America, where some ominous evidence suggests that it may be passed from one person to another.

As the natural ending of the first hantavirus episode demonstrates, ecosystems can usually survive occasional extremes. They are even strengthened by seasonal changes in weather conditions, because the species that live in changeable climates have to evolve an ability to cope with a broad range of conditions. But long-lasting extremes and very wide fluctuations in weather can overwhelm ecosystem resilience. (Persistent ocean heating, for instance, is menacing coral reef systems, and drought-driven forest fires are threatening forest habitats.) And ecosystem upheaval is one of the most profound ways in which climate change can affect human health. Pest control is one of nature's underappreciated services to people; well-functioning ecosystems that include diverse species help to keep nuisance organisms in check. If increased warming and weather extremes result in more ecosystem disturbance, that disruption may foster the growth of opportunist populations and enhance the spread of disease.

Unhealthy Water

Beyond exacerbating the vector-borne illnesses mentioned above, global warming will probably elevate the incidence of waterborne diseases, including cholera (a cause of severe diarrhea). Warming itself can contribute to the change, as can a heightened frequency and extent of droughts and floods. It may seem strange that droughts would favor waterborne disease, but they can wipe out supplies of safe drinking water and concentrate contaminants that might other-wise remain dilute. Further, the lack of clean water during a drought interferes with good hygiene and safe rehydration of those who have lost large amounts of water because of diarrhea or fever.

Floods favor waterborne ills in different ways. They wash sewage and other sources of pathogens (such as *Cryptosporidium*) into supplies of drinking water. They also flush fertilizer into water supplies. Fertilizer and sewage can each combine with warmed water to trigger expansive blooms of harmful algae. Some of these blooms are directly toxic to humans who inhale their vapors; others contaminate fish and shellfish, which, when eaten, sicken the consumers. Recent discoveries have revealed that algal blooms can threaten human health in yet another way. As they grow bigger, they support the proliferation of various pathogens, among them *Vibrio cholerae*, the causative agent of cholera.

Drenching rains brought by a warmed Indian Ocean to the Horn of Africa in 1997 and 1998 offer an example of how people will be affected as global warming spawns added flooding. The downpours set off epidemics of cholera as well as two mosquito-borne infections: malaria and Rift Valley fever (a flulike disease that can be lethal to livestock and people alike).

To the west, Hurricane Mitch stalled over Central America in October 1998 for three days. Fueled by a heated Caribbean, the storm unleashed torrents that killed at least 11,000 people. But that was only the beginning of its havoc. In the aftermath, Honduras reported thousands of cases of cholera, malaria and dengue fever. Beginning in February of this year, unprecedented rains and a series of cyclones inundated large parts of southern Africa. Floods in Mozambique and Madagascar killed hundreds, displaced thousands and spread both cholera and malaria. Such events can also greatly retard economic development, and its accompanying public health benefits, in affected areas for years.

Solutions

The health toll taken by global warming will depend to a large extent on the steps taken to prepare for the dangers. The ideal defensive strategy would have multiple components.

One would include improved surveillance systems that would promptly spot the emergence or resurgence of infectious diseases or the vectors that carry them. Discovery could quickly trigger measures to control vector proliferation without harming the environment, to advise the public about self-protection, to provide vaccines (when available) for at-risk populations and to deliver prompt treatments.

This past spring, efforts to limit the West Nile virus in the northeastern U.S. followed this model. On seeing that the virus had survived the winter, public health officials warned people to clear their yards of receptacles that can hold stagnant water favorable to mosquito breeding. They also introduced fish that eat mosquito larvae into catch basins and put insecticide pellets into sewers.

Sadly, however, comprehensive surveillance plans are not yet realistic in much of the world. And even when vaccines or effective treatments exist, many regions have no means of obtaining and distributing them. Providing these preventive measures and treatments should be a global priority.

A second component would focus on predicting when climatological and other environmental conditions

Weather and West Nile Virus

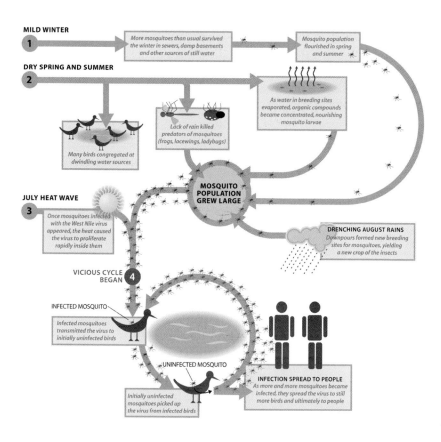

MILD WINTER

1 More mosquitoes than usual survived the winter in sewers, damp basements and other sources of still water → Mosquito population flourished in spring and summer

DRY SPRING AND SUMMER

2

As water in breeding sites evaporated, organic compounds became concentrated, nourishing mosquito larvae

Lack of rain killed predators of mosquitoes (frogs, lacewings, ladybugs)

Many birds congregated at dwindling water sources

MOSQUITO POPULATION GREW LARGE

JULY HEAT WAVE

3 Once mosquitoes infected with the West Nile virus appeared, the heat caused the virus to proliferate rapidly inside them

DRENCHING AUGUST RAINS
Downpours formed new breeding sites for mosquitoes, yielding a new crop of the insects

VICIOUS CYCLE BEGAN 4

INFECTED MOSQUITO

Infected mosquitoes transmitted the virus to initially uninfected birds

UNINFECTED MOSQUITO

Initially uninfected mosquitoes picked up the virus from infected birds

INFECTION SPREAD TO PEOPLE
As more and more mosquitoes became infected, they spread the virus to still more birds and ultimately to people

This diagram offers a possible explanation for how a warming trend and sequential weather extremes helped the West Nile virus to establish itself in the New York City area in 1999. Whether the virus entered the U.S. via mosquitoes, birds or people is unknown. But once it arrived, interactions between mosquitoes and birds amplified its proliferation.

could become conducive to disease outbreaks, so that the risks could be minimized. If climate models indicate that floods are likely in a given region, officials might stock shelters with extra supplies. Or if satellite images and sampling of coastal waters indicate that algal blooms related to cholera outbreaks are beginning, officials could warn people to filter contaminated water and could advise medical facilities to arrange for additional staff, beds and treatment supplies.

Research reported in 1999 illustrates the benefits of satellite monitoring. It showed that satellite images detecting heated water in two specific ocean regions and lush vegetation in the Horn of Africa can predict outbreaks of Rift Valley fever in the Horn five months in advance. If such assessments led to vaccination campaigns in animals, they could potentially forestall epidemics in both livestock and people.

A third component of the strategy would attack global warming itself. Human activities that contribute to the heating or that exacerbate its effects must be limited. Little doubt remains that burning fossil fuels for energy is playing a significant role in global warming, by spewing carbon dioxide and other heat-absorbing, or "greenhouse," gases into the air. Cleaner energy sources must be put to use quickly and broadly, both in the energy-guzzling industrial world and in developing nations, which cannot be expected to cut back on their energy use. (Providing sanitation, housing, food, refrigeration and indoor fires for cooking takes energy, as do the pumping and purification of water and the desalination of seawater for irrigation.) In parallel, forests and wetlands need to be restored, to absorb carbon dioxide and floodwaters and to filter contaminants before they reach water supplies.

The world's leaders, if they are wise, will make it their business to find a way to pay for these solutions. Climate, ecological systems and society can all recoup after stress, but only if they are not exposed to prolonged challenge or to one disruption after another. The Intergovernmental Panel on Climate Change, established by the United Nations, calculates that halting the ongoing rise in atmospheric concentrations of greenhouse gases will require a whopping 60 to 70 percent reduction in emissions.

I worry that effective corrective measures will not be instituted soon enough. Climate does not necessarily change gradually. The multiple factors that are now destabilizing the global climate system could cause it to jump abruptly out of its current state. At any time, the world could suddenly become much hotter or even much colder. Such a sudden, catastrophic change is the ultimate health risk—one that must be avoided at all costs.

Further Information

The Emergence of New Disease. Richard Levins, Tamara Auerbuch, Uwe Brinkmann, Irina Eckardt, Paul R. Epstein, Tim Ford, Najwa Makhoul, Christina dePossas, Charles Puccia, Andrew

Spielman and Mary E. Wilson in *American Scientist*, Vol. 82, No. 1, pages 52–60; January/ February 1994.

Climate Change and Human Health. Edited by Anthony J. McMichael, Andrew Haines, Rudolf Slooff and Sari Kovats. World Health Organization, World Meteorological Organization, United Nations Environmental Program, 1996.

The Regional Impacts of Climate Change: An Assessment of Vulnerability. 1997. Edited by R. T. Watson, M. C. Zinyowera and R. H. Moss. Cambridge University Press, 1997. Summary from the Intergovernmental Panel on Climate Change available at **www.ipcc.ch/pub/reports.htm.**

Biological and Physical Signs of Climate Change: Focus on Mosquito-Borne Diseases. Paul R. Epstein, Henry F. Diaz, Scott Elias, Georg Grabherr, Nicholas E. Graham, Willem J. M. Martens, Ellen Mosley-Thompson and Joel Susskind in *Bulletin of the American Meteorological Society*, Vol. 79, pages 409–417; 1998.

Other Web sites of interest: **www.heatisonline.org** and **www.med.harvard.edu/chge.**

About the Author

PAUL R. EPSTEIN, an M.D. trained in tropical public health, is associate director of the Center for Health and the Global Environment at Harvard Medical School. He has served in medical, teaching and research capacities in Africa, Asia and Latin America and has worked with the Intergovernmental Panel on Climate Change, the National Oceanic and Atmospheric Administration, and the National Aeronautics and Space Administration to assess the health effects of climate change and to develop health applications for climate forecasting and remote-sensing technologies.

6. "On Thin Ice?"

By Robert A. Bindschadler and Charles R. Bentley

How soon humanity will have to move inland to escape rising seas depends in great part on how quickly West Antarctica's massive ice sheet shrinks. Scientists are finally beginning to agree on what controls the size of the sheet and its rate of disintegration.

Twelve thousand years ago, as the earth emerged from the last ice age, vast armadas of *Titanic*-size icebergs invaded the North Atlantic. Purged vigorously from the enormous ice sheets that smothered half of North America and Europe at the time, those icebergs displaced enough water to raise global sea level more than a meter a year for decades.

As the frozen north melted, the ice gripping the planet's southernmost continent remained essentially intact and now represents 90 percent of the earth's solid water. But dozens of scientific studies conducted over the past 30 years have warned that the ice blanketing West Antarctica—the part lying mainly in the Western Hemisphere—could repeat the dramatic acts of its northern cousins. Holding more than three million cubic kilometers of freshwater in its frozen clutches, this ice sheet would raise global sea level five meters (about 16 feet) if it were to disintegrate completely, swamping myriad coastal lowlands and forcing many of their two billion inhabitants to retreat inland.

Most Antarctic scientists have long concurred that the continent's ice has shrunk in the past, contributing to a rise in sea level that continued even after the northern ice sheets were gone. The experts also agree that the ice covering the eastern side of the continent is remarkably stable relative to that in West Antarctica, where critical differences in the underlying terrain make it inherently more erratic. But until quite recently, they disagreed over the likelihood of a catastrophic breakup of the western ice sheet in the near future. Many, including one of us (Bindschadler), worried that streams of ice flowing from the continent's interior toward the Ross Sea might undermine the sheet's integrity, leading to its total collapse in a few centuries or less. Others (including Bentley) pointed to the sheet's recent persistence, concluding that the sheet is reasonably stable.

For a time it seemed the debate might never be resolved. Agreement was hampered by scant data and the challenge of studying a continent shrouded half

Overview/Antartic Ice

- For nearly three decades, numerous Antarctic experts warned that West Antarctica's ice sheet is in the midst of a rapid disintegration that could raise global sea level five meters in a few centuries or less.
- Many of those researchers now think that the ice sheet is shrinking much more slowly than they originally suspected and that sea level is more likely to rise half a meter or less in the next century.
- That consensus is not without its caveats. The ice sheet's poorly understood Amundsen sector now appears to be shrinking faster than previously thought.
- Global warming, which has so far played a negligible role in West Antarctica's fate, is bound to wield greater influence in the future.

the year in frigid darkness. In addition, although areas of the ice sheet have drained quickly in the past, it is difficult to determine whether changes in the size or speed of the ice seen today are a reflection of normal variability or the start of a dangerous trend. In the past few years, though, a variety of field and laboratory studies have yielded a growing consensus on the forces controlling West Antarctica's future, leading experts in both camps to conclude that the ice streams pointing toward the Ross Sea are not currently as threatening as some of us had feared.

We remain puzzled, however, over the ice sheet's ultimate fate. New studies have revealed thinning ice in a long-neglected sector of West Antarctica, suggesting that a destructive process other than ice streams is operating there. And another region—the peninsula that forms Antarctica's northernmost arm—has recently experienced warmer summer temperatures that are almost certainly the reason behind an ongoing breakup of ice along its coasts.

Around the world temperatures have risen gradually since the end of the last ice age, but the trend has accelerated markedly since the mid-1990s with the increase of heat-trapping greenhouse gases in the atmosphere. So far the peninsula seems to be the only part of Antarctica where this recent climate trend has left its mark; average temperatures elsewhere have risen less or even cooled slightly in the past 50 years. Researchers are now scrambling to determine whether

Past, Present and Future?

Antarctica's thick blanket of ice *(below)* has been contracting, mostly gradually but sometimes swiftly, since the height of the last ice age, 20,000 years ago. The greatest reduction has occurred in West Antarctica, where the ice sheet is considerably more fragile than its counterpart in the east. Because the western sheet has changed quickly in the past, scientists have been unsure whether recent dramatic ice losses reflect normal variability or the start of an ominous trend toward total collapse. In the wake of a catastrophic collapse, rapidly rising seas would flood coastal communities around the world.

—R.A.B. and C.R.B

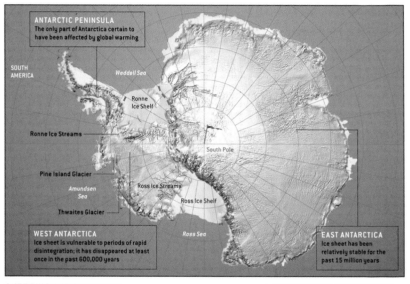

ANTARCTIC PENINSULA
The only part of Antarctica certain to have been affected by global warming

SOUTH AMERICA

Weddell Sea

Ronne Ice Shelf

Ronne Ice Streams

South Pole

Pine Island Glacier

Amundsen Sea

Ross Ice Streams

Ross Ice Shelf

Thwaites Glacier

WEST ANTARCTICA
Ice sheet is vulnerable to periods of rapid disintegration; it has disappeared at least once in the past 600,000 years

Ross Sea

EAST ANTARCTICA
Ice sheet has been relatively stable for the past 15 million years

SHEDDING AND SHRINKING

CHANGE IN ICE THICKNESS since the last ice age *(right)* translates into a loss of about 5.3. million cubic kilometers, much of it from West Antartica. The ice sheet's grounded edge, that reaching the seafloor, has shrunk particularly rapidly in the Ross Sea over the past 7,000 years, retreating some 700 kilometers inland.

ROSS ICE STREAMS

PRESENT DAY

3,200 YEARS AGO

6,800 YEARS AGO

EDGE OF GROUNDED ICE 20,000 YEARS AGO

2,600 YEARS AGO

ROSS SEA

0   kilometers   500

THE WORST-CASE SCENARIO

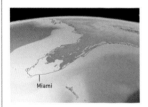

Miami

COMPLETE COLLAPSE of West Antarctica's ice sheet would raise sea level five meters. Among the casualties would be southern Florida *(above)*, where about a third of the famous peninsula would disappear under-water. Today West Antarctica contributes about 10 percent of the average sea-level rise of two millimeters a year.

global warming is poised to gain a broader foothold at the bottom of the world.

Early Alarms

Indications that the West Antarctic ice sheet might be in the midst of a vanishing act first began cropping up about 30 years ago. In 1974 Johannes Weertman of Northwestern University published one of the most influential early studies, a theoretical analysis of West Antarctica based on the forces then thought to control the stability of ice sheets. By that time scientists were well aware that most of the land underlying the thick ice in West Antarctica sits far below sea level and once constituted the floor of an ocean. If all the ice were to become liquid, a mountainous landscape would appear, with valleys dipping more than two kilometers below the surface of the sea and peaks climbing two kilometers above it. Because the boundaries of West Antarctica are so sunken, ice at the edges makes extensive contact with the surrounding seawater, and a good deal extends—as floating ice shelves—onto the ocean surface.

Weertman's troubling conclusion was that any ice sheet that fills a marine basin is inherently unstable when global sea level is on the rise, which most scientists agree has been the case for the past 20,000 years. This instability arises because the edges of a marine ice sheet can be easily stressed or even lifted off the underlying sediment by the natural buoyant effects of water. (In contrast, the ice sheet in East Antarctica sits on a

Chilly Realities

Predicting Antarctic ice sheets' response to changing climate and their influence on sea level is not always straightforward. Here are a few of the less obvious phenomena that scientists must take into account:

Ice need not melt to add to rising seas

Ice that was once on land contributes to global sea level as soon as it begins floating. Indeed, an iceberg—most of which sits below the ocean surface—is already displacing as much seawater as it will in liquid form. The same is true for ice shelves, the floating

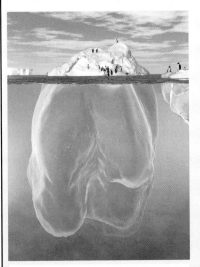

tongues of ice that extend seaward from the edges of continents. In Antarctica, frigid temperatures—averaging about −34 degrees Celsius (−29 degrees Fahrenheit)—mean that very little of that continent's ice ever melts. That might change if global warming becomes more pervasive in the region, but at present Antarctica influences sea level only when solid ice, which is delivered to the coasts by coastal glaciers or by other natural conveyor belts called ice streams, breaks off or adds to existing ice shelves.

Floating iceberg belies its true size when viewed from above. Ninety percent of its mass lurks below the surface.

Ice can either accelerate or counteract the effects of global warming

Think of a snowy field in the bright sun. Ice and snow reflect much more solar energy back to space than dark oceans and land surfaces do. Such reflection tends to enable an already cold part of the atmosphere above the ice to stay cool, increasing the likelihood that more ice will form.

On the other hand, if global warming heats the atmosphere enough to begin melting the ice and exposing more of the darker surface below, then the region will absorb more solar energy and the air will become warmer still.

Global warming could either slow the rise of sea level or speed it up

Warmer air increases evaporation from the oceans and carries more moisture than cooler air does. So as global warming increases, more evaporated seawater from temperate areas could be transported to polar areas, where it would fall as snow. This process would be further enhanced if global warming were to melt significant amounts of sea ice and expose more of the ocean surface to the atmosphere. All else being equal, ocean water could be preserved as snow faster than it would reenter the sea, alleviating some of the rise in sea level. The catch is that global warming can also cause land ice to melt or break apart more quickly. The ultimate effect of global warming on ice sheets depends on which process dominates.

—R.A.B. and C.R.B

continent, most of which rests high above the deleterious influence of the sea.) The outcome of Weertman's simple calculation was that West Antarctica's ice sheet was on a course toward total collapse. Nothing short of a new ice age could alter this fate.

If Weertman's thinking was correct, it meant that the modern ice sheet was already a shrunken version of its former self. Many early discoveries lent support to this conclusion. Explorers found unusual piles of rock and debris (which only moving ice could have created) on mountain slopes high above the present surface of the ice, indicating that the ice was once much thicker. Likewise, deep gouges carved in the seafloor off the coast implied that the grounded edge of the ice sheet (the part resting on the seafloor) once extended farther out into the ocean [see "Past, Present and Future?" box]. Based on these kinds of limited observations, some researchers estimated that the ice sheet was originally as much as three times its present volume and that it was shrinking fairly slowly—at a rate that would lead to its complete disappearance in another 4,000 to 7,000 years.

The idea that West Antarctica could lurch much more rapidly toward collapse was not formulated until researchers started paying close attention to ice streams—natural conveyor belts hundreds of kilometers long and dozens of kilometers wide. Early investigators inferred that these streams owe their existence in part to tectonic forces that are pulling West Antarctica apart, thinning the crust and allowing an above-average amount of the earth's internal heat to escape. This extra warmth from below could melt the base of the ice sheet, providing a lubricated layer that would allow the ice to move rapidly down even the gentlest of slopes. Indeed, airborne surveys using ice-penetrating radar revealed in the 1970s that two networks of ice streams drain ice from the continent's interior and feed it to West Antarctica's two largest ice shelves, the Ross and the Ronne. As the ice reaches the seaward edge of these shelves, it eventually calves off as huge icebergs. As this dynamic picture of ice streams came to light, so did the first warnings that they harbored the potential to drain the entire ice sheet in a few centuries or less.

Streams of Uncertainty

Driven by the new knowledge that the fate of the West Antarctic ice sheet would depend strongly on how fast these streams were removing ice from the continent, teams from NASA, Ohio State University and the University of Wisconsin–Madison set up summer research camps on and near the ice streams in 1983. Some scientists probed the interior of the streams with radar and seismic explosions; others measured their motion and deformation at the surface. They quickly found that these immense rivers race along at glaciologically breakneck speeds—at hundreds of meters a year, many times faster than the average mountain glacier.

Different field investigators sought explanations for the speed of the streams by melting narrow, kilometer-long holes through the ice to extract samples of the ancient seafloor below. Ground-up shells of marine organisms mixed with pebbles, clay and eroded rock, deposited there over many millennia, now form a bed of muddy paste that is so soft and well lubricated that the ice streams can glide along even more easily than earlier researchers expected. If they had instead found crystalline rock, like that underlying most continental ice sheets, including East Antarctica's, they would have concluded that the greater friction of that material had been inhibiting ice motion.

These realizations left wide open the possibility of swift drainage along the Ross ice streams. In contrast, British workers who were studying the Ronne ice streams on the other side of West Antarctica reassured the world that the prospects were not nearly so grim in their sector. But the scientists camped out near the Ross

Ice Shelf had reason to believe that once the Ross ice streams carried away that region's one million cubic kilometers of ice, the rest of the sheet—including the area drained by the Ronne streams and part of the East Antarctic ice sheet—would surely follow.

In the 1990s researchers began to notice another potentially unsettling characteristic of the Ross ice streams: they are not only fast but fickle. Radar examinations of the hidden structure below the surface of the grounded ice revealed that the ice streams were not always in their present locations. Satellite imagery of the Ross Ice Shelf, which is composed of ice that has arrived over the past 1,000 years, discovered crevasses and other features that serve as a natural record of dramatic and unmistakable changes in the streams' rates of flow. Indeed, one stream known simply as "C" apparently stopped flowing suddenly a century and a half ago. Similarly, the Whillans ice stream has been decelerating over the past few decades. If the streams do come and go, as such findings implied, then their future would be much more difficult to predict than once assumed. The most alarming possibility was that the stagnant streams might start flowing again without warning. But reassurance against that prospect, at least for the near future, was soon to come.

About five years ago a slew of reports began providing key evidence that the ice sheet may not have thinned as much as previously estimated. In 2000 Eric J. Steig of the University of Washington used new techniques to analyze an old ice core recovered in 1968

Slip Sliding Away

Immense ice streams shuttle ice to West Antarctica's coasts at speeds of hundreds of meters a year, feeding more than 400 cubic kilometers to ice shelves annually. They could thus drain the ice sheet in 7,000 years or less if snowfall did not replenish it. Reassuring findings indicate, however, that the streams can stagnate for long periods. Whether they stop or go depends on how much liquid water exists at the base of the ice: a lot makes a stream move quickly; too little slows it down.

—R.A.B. and C.R.B

Ice streams glide swiftly when the muddy till below them becomes wet. Water forms when the earth's internal heat warms the bottom of the ice. Because the thick overlying ice insulates the deeper layers from the cold atmosphere, the till becomes warm enough to melt the base of the stream. Meltwater then seeps into the till, which becomes extremely soft and smears easily under the weight of the overlying ice.

Ice streams stagnate suddenly when water becomes scarce. As ice flows rapidly, it thins, allowing the frigidity of the air to penetrate it more deeply. As the ice closer to the till cools, the earth's heat escapes more quickly toward the surface and has no time to melt ice at the base. This heat loss freezes the water in the till, making it stiff and sticky. Unless water from upstream keeps the till pliable, the stream grinds to a halt.

from the heart of West Antarctica. The initial analysis had indicated that the ice was 950 meters higher during the last ice age than it is today, but Steig's improved interpretation reduced that difference to 200 meters. In the mountains of the Executive Committee Range,

John O. Stone, another University of Washington researcher, clocked the thinning of the ice sheet by measuring the radioactive by-products of cosmic rays, which have decayed at a known rate since the moment when ice retreat left rock outcrops freshly exposed. These observations put severe limits on the original size of the ice sheet, suggesting that it could have been no more than two and a half times as large as it is today.

By early 2001 scientists on both sides of the debate over the future of West Antarctica's ice sheet were still able to maintain their points of view. Reconciling solid but contradictory evidence required everyone to recognize that great variability on shorter timescales can also appear as lesser variability on longer timescales. Since then, improved measurements of the motion of the Ross ice streams have confirmed that new snowfall is generally keeping pace with ice loss in this sector, meaning that almost no overall shrinkage is occurring at present. And by late 2001 most Antarctic scientists— including both of us—could finally agree that the Ross ice streams are not causing the ice to thin at this time. Variations in snowfall versus ice discharge over the past millennium seem to have averaged out—a sign that the ice sheet is less likely to make sudden additions to rising seas than some investigators had expected.

But scientists engaged in this debate know all too well that the dynamic nature of the ice streams dictates that this reconciliation explains only what is going on today. Looking further back in time, for instance, geologic evidence near the U.S. McMurdo Station suggests that the ice sheet retreated through that area very rapidly around 7,000 years ago. Thus, even if not sustained, this type of regional collapse may have occurred during brief periods and could happen again.

To gain a better handle on the future stability of the ice sheet, researchers have also developed a firmer understanding of the forces that control the flow of ice within streams, including an explanation for why the streams can stop, start and change velocity on different timescales [see "Slip Sliding Away" box]. It turns out that sediment (also called till) and water in the seabed are in control over days and years, but global climate, principally through air temperature and sea level, dominates over millennia. This and other new information will make it possible to build more reliable computer models of how the streams might behave centuries hence.

Weak Underbelly Exposed

That the area of the West Antarctic ice sheet drained by the Ross ice streams is in less danger of imminent collapse is good news. But in the past couple of years it has become clear that not all sections of West Antarctica behave in the same way. While field-workers were concentrating their efforts on the ice streams feeding the Ross and Ronne ice shelves, several satellite sensors were patiently collecting data from another sector of the ice sheet, the poorly understood region adjacent to the Amundsen Sea. There groups from the U.S. and Great Britain have discovered that the glaciers in this mysterious area are disappearing at an even faster rate than had been originally hypothesized for the Ross ice streams.

After poring over millions of ice-elevation measurements made from space during the 1980s and 1990s, Duncan J. Wingham of University College London and H. Jay Zwally of the NASA Goddard Space Flight Center showed independently that the parts of the ice sheet that feed the Pine Island and Thwaites glaciers are thinning, the latter at more than 10 centimeters a year. These results mesh beautifully with another recent report, by Eric Rignot of the Jet Propulsion Laboratory in Pasadena, Calif. Using radar interferometry, a technique capable of detecting ice movement as small as a few millimeters, Rignot observed that both glaciers are delivering ice increasingly quickly to the Amundsen Sea *and* shrinking toward the continent's interior. As a result, they currently contribute between 0.1 and 0.2 millimeter a year to global sea-level rise—up to 10 percent of the total. At that rate these glaciers would drain 30 percent of the total ice sheet in 7,500 to 15,000 years, or much faster if a catastrophe like the one hypothesized earlier for the Ross sector were to occur.

This new evidence is no surprise to glaciologists such as Terence J. Hughes of the University of Maine, who long ago dubbed the Amundsen sector "the weak underbelly of the West Antarctic ice sheet." But logistical limitations have discouraged field observations in this remote region for decades—it is far from any permanent research station and is renowned as one of the cloudiest regions on the earth. In addition, unique qualities of the Amundsen Sea glaciers may mean that the hard-won knowledge from the Ross sector will be inapplicable there. The surfaces of the glaciers slope more steeply toward the sea than do the ice streams, for example. And because the glaciers dump their ice directly into the sea instead of adding ice to an existing ice shelf, some scientists have argued that this region may be further along in the disintegration process than any other part of Antarctica.

Turning Up the Heat

Uncertainty over the vulnerability of the Amundsen Sea sector is but one of several unknowns that scientists still must address. Increasing temperatures related to global warming could begin creeping toward the South Pole from the Antarctic Peninsula, where the summer-time atmosphere has already warmed by more than two degrees C since the 1950s. Even seemingly subtle changes in air temperature could trigger disintegration of ice shelves that are relatively stable at present. Evidence reported this year also suggests that warmer ocean waters mixing from lower latitudes may be melting the ice sheet's grounded edges faster than previously assumed, along with reducing the amount of ice in the Amundsen Sea.

Conveniently for those of us living in the world today, the West Antarctic ice sheet appears to possess more helpful feedbacks—such as those that can cause fast-moving ice streams to stagnate for centuries on end—than either its North American or European cousins long gone. Their destruction occurred suddenly as a result of a few degrees of warming, and yet much of West Antarctica's ice survived. Weertman's early model seems to have oversimplified the ice sheet's own dynamics, which so far have exerted enough control over its size to avoid, or at least forestall, a swift demise.

Based on what we know so far, we predict—albeit cautiously—that the ice sheet will continue shrinking, but only over thousands of years. If that is correct, West Antarctica's average effect on sea level could be roughly double its historic contribution of two millimeters a year. That means this ice sheet would add another meter to sea level only every 500 years. But before anyone breathes a sigh of relief, we must remember that this remarkable ice sheet has been surprising researchers for more than 30 years—and could have more shocks in store.

More to Explore

Rapid Sea-Level Rise Soon from West Antarctic Ice-Sheet Collapse? Charles R. Bentley in *Science*, Vol. 275, pages 1077–1078; February 21, 1997.

Future of the West Antarctic Ice Sheet. Robert
   Bindschadler in *Science*, Vol. 282, pages 428–429;
   October 16, 1998.

The West Antarctic Ice Sheet: Behavior and
   Environment. Edited by Richard B. Alley and
   Robert A. Bindschadler. Antarctic Research Series,
   Vol. 77. American Geophysical Union, 2001.

West Antarctic research program Web site: **www.
   glacier.rice.edu.**

About the Authors

ROBERT A. BINDSCHADLER and *CHARLES R.
BENTLEY* have devoted most of their research careers
to investigating the West Antarctic ice sheet and the
continent below it. In 23 years at the NASA Goddard
Space Flight Center, Bindschadler has led 12 field
expeditions to the frozen land down under. Now a
senior research fellow at Goddard, he has developed
numerous remote-sensing technologies for glaciological
application—measuring ice velocity and elevation using
satellite imagery and monitoring melting of the ice sheet
by microwave emissions, to name just two. Bentley's first
visit to West Antarctica lasted 25 months, during which
he led an exploratory traverse of the ice sheet as part of
the 1957–58 International Geophysical Year expedition.
He returned regularly as a member of the geophysics
faculty at the University of Wisconsin–Madison until
his retirement in 1998.

7. "Meltdown in the North"

By Matthew Sturm, Donald K. Perovich
and Mark C. Serreze

Sea ice and glaciers are melting, permafrost is thawing, tundra is yielding to shrubs—and scientists are struggling to understand how these changes will affect not just the Arctic but the entire planet.

Snow crystals sting my face and coat my beard and the ruff of my parka. As the wind rises, it becomes difficult to see my five companions through the blowing snow. We are 500 miles into a 750-mile snowmobile trip across Arctic Alaska. We have come, in the late winter of 2002, to measure the thickness of the snow cover and estimate its insulating capacity, an important factor in maintaining the thermal balance of the permafrost. I have called a momentary halt to decide what to do. The rising wind, combined with -30 degree Fahrenheit temperatures, makes it clear we need to find shelter, and fast. I put my face against the hood of my nearest companion and shout: "Make sure everyone stays close together. We have to get off this exposed ridge."

At the time, the irony that we might freeze to death while looking for evidence of global warming was lost on me, but later, snug in our tents, I began to laugh at how incongruous that would have been.

—Matthew Sturm

The list is impressively long: The warmest air temperatures in four centuries, a shrinking sea-ice cover, a record amount of melting on the Greenland Ice Sheet, Alaskan glaciers retreating at unprecedented rates. Add to this the increasing discharge from Russian rivers, an Arctic growing season that has lengthened by several days per decade, and permafrost that has started to thaw. Taken together, these observations announce in a way no single measurement could that the Arctic is undergoing a profound transformation. Its full extent has come to light only in the past decade, after scientists in different disciplines began comparing their findings. Now many of those scientists are collaborating, trying to understand the ramifications of the changes and to predict what lies ahead for the Arctic and the rest of the globe.

What they learn will have planetwide importance because the Arctic exerts an outsize degree of control on the climate. Much as a spillway in a dam controls the level of a reservoir, the polar regions control the earth's heat balance. Because more solar energy is absorbed in the tropics than at the poles, winds and ocean currents constantly transport heat poleward, where the extensive snow and ice cover influences its fate. As long as this highly reflective cover is intact and extensive, sunlight coming directly into the Arctic is mostly reflected back into space, keeping the Arctic cool and a good repository for the heat brought in from lower latitudes. But if the cover begins to melt and shrink, it will reflect less sunlight, and the Arctic

Overview/Arctic Warming

- Signs of warming are everywhere in the Arctic, and these changes are bound to affect conditions on the rest of the planet because the polar regions exert an outsize control on the earth's heat balance.
- A complex web of climatic feedback systems makes it extremely difficult to know whether greenhouse warming is the primary cause of the transformation in the Arctic.
- But whatever is causing the changes, scientists face the urgent task of predicting what lies ahead rather than waiting to react to the consequences as they unfold.

will become a poorer repository, eventually warming the climate of the entire planet.

Figuring out just what will happen, however, is fraught with complications. The greatest of these stems from the intricate feedback systems that govern the climate in the Arctic. Some of these processes are positive, amplifying change and turning a nudge into a shove, and some are negative, behaving as a brake on the system and mitigating change.

Chief among these processes is the ice-albedo feedback [see "A Complex Web" box], in which rising temperatures produce shorter winters and less extensive snow and ice cover, with ripple effects all the way back through the midlatitudes. Another feedback is associated with the large stores of carbon frozen into the Arctic in the form of peat. As the climate warms and this peat thaws, it could release carbon dioxide into the atmosphere and enhance warming over not just the Arctic but the whole globe—a phenomenon commonly referred to as greenhouse warming.

The key problem is that we don't fully understand how some of these feedback processes work in isolation, let alone how they interact. What we do know is that the Arctic is a complex system: change one thing, and everything else responds, sometimes in a counterintuitive way.

Heating Up

The more we look, the more change we see. Arctic air temperatures have increased by 0.5 degree Celsius each decade over the past 30 years, with most of the warming coming in winter and spring. Proxy records (ice and peat cores, lake sediments), which tell us mostly about summer temperatures, put this recent warming in perspective. They indicate that late 20th- and early 21st-century temperatures are at their highest level in 400 years. The same records tell us that these high levels are the result of steady warming for 100 years as the Arctic emerged from the Little Ice Age, a frigid period that ended around 1850, topped off by a dramatic acceleration of the warming in the past half a century.

The recent temperature trends are mirrored in many other time series. One example is that Arctic and Northern Hemisphere river and lake ice has been forming later and melting earlier since the Little Ice Age. The total ice-cover season is 16 days shorter than it was in 1850. Near one of our homes (Sturm's) in Alaska, a jackpot of about $300,000 awaits the person who can guess the date the Tanana River will break up every spring. The average winning date has gotten earlier by about six days since the betting pool was instituted in 1917. Higher-tech data—satellite images—show that the snow-free season in the Arctic has lengthened by several days each decade since the early 1970s. Similarly, the growing season has increased by as much as four days.

Shrinking Glaciers, Thawing Permafrost

There was nothing complex about my first research in Arctic climate change: march around a small glacier on Ellesmere Island, drill holes in the ice, insert long metal poles in the holes, measure them, come back a year later and see if more pole was showing.

We put in most of the pole network in the warm summer of 1982 and returned in 1983 to a very different world—week after week of cold, snow and fog. It looked like the start of a new ice age. Our plan had been to go back annually, but as so often happens, funding dried up, and my Arctic experiences became fond memories.

But memories sometimes get refreshed. In 2002 I got a call from an excited graduate student. He had revisited the glacier. It was rapidly wasting away. 1983 had been an anomaly. My stakes were there, except they were all lying on the surface of the ice. How deeply had I installed them? Did I still have my field notes? He need not have worried. There was my field book, dusty but safe in my bookcase. Now I'm going back to Ellesmere Island, to see what's left of the glacier that in 1983 seemed like such a permanent feature of the landscape but that I now realize may well die before I do.

—*Mark C. Serreze*

Arctic glaciers tell a striking tale as well. In Alaska, they have been shrinking for five decades, and more startlingly, the rate of shrinkage has increased threefold in the past 10 years. The melting glaciers translate into a rise in sea level of about two millimeters a decade, or 10 percent of the total annual rise of 20 millimeters. Determining the state of the much larger and more slowly changing Greenland Ice Sheet has been something of a Holy Grail for Arctic researchers. Older field and satellite results suggested that the ice sheet was exhibiting asymmetrical behavior—the west side thinning in a modest way and the east side remaining in balance. Recent satellite images indicate that the melt rate over the entire ice sheet has been increasing with time. The total area melting in a given summer has increased by 7 percent each decade since 1978, with last summer setting an all-time record. Winter snowfall appears insufficient to offset this heavy summer melt, so the sheet is shrinking.

The permafrost—the permanently frozen layer below the surface—is thawing, too. In a study published in 1986, researchers from the U.S. Geological Survey carefully logged temperature profiles in deep oil-exploration boreholes drilled through the permafrost of northern Alaska. When they extrapolated the profiles to the surface, they found an anomalous curvature that was best explained by a warming at ground level of two to four degrees C during the preceding few decades. More recently, preliminary results suggest an additional increase of two to three degrees C has occurred since 1986. Because the Arctic winter lasts nine months of the year, snow cover controls the thermal state of the ground as much as air temperature does, so these borehole records almost certainly reflect a change in the amount and timing of winter precipitation as well as an increase in temperature. More snow means thicker insulation and therefore better protection for the ground from frigid winter temperatures. Ground that is not chilled as much in the winter is primed for more warming in the summer.

Regardless of why it is occurring, one thing is certain. Thawing permafrost is trouble. It can produce catastrophic failure of roads, houses and other infra-structure. It is also implicated in another recently detected change: over the past 60 years, the discharge of freshwater from Russian rivers into the Arctic Basin has increased by 7 percent—an amount equivalent to roughly one quarter the volume of Lake Erie or three months of the outflow of the Mississippi River. Scientists attribute the change partly to greater winter precipitation and partly to a warming of the permafrost and active layer, which they believe is now transporting more groundwater. This influx of freshwater could have important implications for global climate: the paleo-record suggests that when the outflow of water from the Arctic Basin hits a critical level of freshness, the global ocean circulation changes dramatically. When ocean circulation changes, climate does as well, because the circulation system—essentially a set of moving rivers of water in the ocean, such as the Gulf Stream—is one of the prime conveyors of heat northward toward the pole.

Greening of the Arctic

The Arctic land cover is also shifting. Based on warming experiments using greenhouses, biologists have known for some time that shrubs will grow at the expense of the other tundra plants when the climate warms. Under the same favorable growing conditions, the tree line will migrate north. Researchers have been looking for these modifications in the real world, but ecosystem responses can be slow. Only in the past few years, by comparing modern photographs with ones taken 50 years ago, and by using satellites to detect the increasing amount of leaf area, have researchers been able to document that both types of transformations are under way. As the vegetation alters, so does the role of the Arctic in the global carbon cycle. Vast stores of carbon in the form of peat underlie much of the tundra in Alaska and Russia, evidence that for long periods Arctic tundra has been a net carbon sink; about 600 cubic miles of peat are currently in cold storage. In recent years, warming has produced a shift: the Arctic now appears to be a net source of carbon dioxide. The change is subtle but troubling because carbon dioxide and methane constitute the primary greenhouse gases in the atmosphere, returning heat to the earth instead of allowing it to escape into space.

Warmer winters have driven some of the shift. When the air is warmer, more precipitation falls from the sky, some of it coming as snow. The thicker snow holds more warmth in the earth, resulting in a longer period during which the tundra is releasing carbon dioxide. But as the tundra becomes shrubbier and as the soil becomes drier in the summer as a result of higher temperatures, the balance could swing back the other way, because plants, particularly woody ones, will fix more carbon and lock it back into the Arctic ecosystem. The most recent studies suggest, in fact, that the magnitude and direction of the Arctic carbon balance depend on the time span that we are examining, with the response varying as the plants adapt to the new conditions.

Melting Sea Ice

"This sea ice is ridiculously thin," I thought as I broke through the ice for the second time that morning in August 1998. There was no real danger, now that personal flotation devices had become the de rigueur fashion accessory, but the thin ice was troubling for other reasons.

My journey to this place, 600 miles from the North Pole, had begun 10 months earlier on board the icebreaker Des Groseilliers, *which we had intentionally frozen into the pack to begin a yearlong drift. Our mission was to study ice-albedo and cloud-radiation feedbacks. When we started the journey, I was surprised at how thin the ice was. Now, after a much longer than expected summer melt season, it was thinner still, even though we had been drifting steadily north. I was uncertain which would come first: the end of the summer or the end of the ice. Little did I know that this summer the record for minimum ice cover was being set throughout the entire western Arctic Ocean. Unfortunately for the long-term survival of the ice pack, it was a record that was easily broken in 2002.*

—Donald K. Perovich

A Complex Web

The many feedback systems operating in the Arctic make predicting the future state of the region a challenge. The ice-albedo feedback is the granddaddy of all these systems. It works this way: land, ocean and ice reflect a fraction of the incoming sunlight, which consequently escapes into space and does not contribute to heating the climate. This fraction is called the albedo. A surface with an albedo of 1 reflects all light, and a surface with an albedo of 0 reflects none. Strikingly, the Arctic Ocean spans nearly this entire range. Where it is frozen and snow-covered, it has the highest albedo of any naturally occurring material, about 0.85, but where it is ice-free, it has the lowest, around 0.07.

In late spring the ice pack is snow-covered—bright and white. The surface reflects most, but not quite all, of the incident sunlight. Some of the ice melts, causing the ice edge to retreat and replacing the bright, highly reflecting snow-covered ice with the dark, absorbing ocean water. Moreover, away from the ocean's edge, melting snow produces ponds of water that also have a low albedo. Melting in both these areas decreases the albedo, which leads to even greater melting, and so on and on.

If the ice-albedo feedback operated in isolation, predicting its ramifications on global climate might be possible even now. But it does not. Instead multiple feedbacks, some positive and some negative, work in concert, and their net effect is difficult to assess. For example, if the albedo is reduced, the effect is to warm the climate, but then the atmosphere can hold more water vapor, and cloud cover will increase. Clouds act as an umbrella that reduces the amount of sunlight reaching the surface (resulting in cooling), but they also trap long-wave radiation from the surface like a blanket (resulting in warming). In the winter the effect is clear—no sunlight, no umbrella, only the blanket. The cloud feedback is positive.

But what about in summer, when sunlight is plentiful? Field studies have shown that the feedback depends on the nature of the clouds. For high, thin clouds composed primarily of ice, the umbrella effect dominated and the cloud-radiation feedback was negative. But for the low, liquid-water clouds that are prevalent in the summer, the blanket dominated and the feedback was positive. Indeed, when these low clouds were present, more ice melted than on sunny days.

Scientists are now trying to sort out which of the feedbacks in the complex web that constitutes the Arctic are the ones we need to worry about the most. These are the ones—such as the ice-albedo feedback—that can amplify changes already under way, speeding them up and magnifying them. They are the ones that can push the system over the edge.

—M.S., D.K.P. and M.C.S.

Of all the changes we have catalogued, the most alarming by far has been the reduction in the Arctic sea-ice cover. Researchers tracking this alteration have discovered that the area covered by the ice has been decreasing by about 3 percent each decade since the advent of satellite records in 1972. This rate might be low for a financial investment, but where time is measured in centuries or millennia, it is high. With the sea ice covering an area approximately the size of the U.S., the reduction per decade is equivalent to an area the size of Colorado and New Hampshire combined, the home states of two of us (Perovich and Serreze). The change in the thickness of the ice (determined from submarines) is even more striking: as much as 40 percent lost in the past few decades. Some climate models suggest that by 2080 the Arctic Ocean will be ice-free in summer.

The melting sea ice does not raise sea level as melting glaciers do, because the ice is already floating, but it is alarming for two other reasons. Locally, the demise of the sea ice leads to the loss of a unique marine ecosystem replete with polar bears, seals and whales. Globally, an ice-free Arctic Ocean would be the extreme end point of the ice-albedo feedback—far more solar radiation would be absorbed, warming not just the Arctic but eventually every part of the earth.

The shrinking sea-ice cover has not escaped the attention of businesspeople, tourists and politicians. Serious discussions have been under way about the

feasibility of transporting cargo via Arctic waters—
including through the fabled Northwest Passage,
now perhaps close to being a practical shipping route
because of climate change. Roald Amundsen, the
redoubtable Norwegian polar explorer, took more
than three years to complete the first transit of the
passage in 1906, when the Arctic was still under the
influence of the Little Ice Age. Many explorers before
him had died trying to make the journey. In the past
few years, however, dozens of ships have completed
the route, including Russian icebreakers refurbished
for the tourist trade. These events would have been
unimaginable, even with icebreakers, in the more
intense ice conditions of 100 years ago.

Is Greenhouse Warming the Culprit?

This inventory of startling transformation in the Arctic
inevitably raises the question of whether we are still
emerging from the Little Ice Age or whether something
quite different is now taking place. Specifically, should
we interpret these changes as being caused by the
increased concentration of atmospheric greenhouse
gases overriding a natural temperature cycle? Or are
they part of a longer-than-expected natural cycle?

The intricate web of feedback interactions renders
this question exceedingly complicated—and we
don't know enough yet to answer it unequivocally.
But we know enough to be very worried.

Winds of Change

Even in the days of the Vikings, people knew that when winters in northern Europe were mild, they tended to be severe in southern Greenland, and vice versa. Today we know that this seesaw in temperature affects more than just Greenland and Europe. It is related to an atmospheric circulation pattern known as the North Atlantic Oscillation (NAO, which may be part of an even larger pattern, the Arctic Oscillation, or AO). The NAO describes the linked variation of a major low pressure area centered near Iceland with a major high pressure area centered near the Azores. When both pressure features are strong, the NAO is in its positive mode. When both are weak, it is in its negative mode.

A key feature of the NAO is that winds blow counterclockwise around the Icelandic Low, while they blow clockwise around the Azores High. In positive mode, the winds around the Icelandic Low are stronger than normal and warm air from the south streams over northern Europe and northern Eurasia. At the same time, the circulation pattern sweeps cold air down from the high Arctic over parts of Greenland, the North Atlantic and northeastern North America. When the NAO is negative, the wind pattern weakens (and at times can even reverse), which leads to roughly the opposite temperature pattern. Since about 1970, the winter NAO has been largely "stuck" in its positive mode, which helps to explain why we have observed widespread warming over Alaska, western Canada and Eurasia but regional cooling in eastern Canada and southern Greenland. The pattern has also caused increased precipitation in northern Eurasia and contributed to the reduction in sea ice.

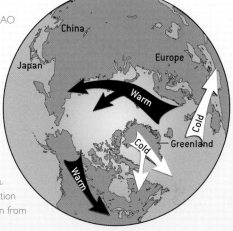

North Atlantic Oscillation is depicted in its positive mode.

—M.S., D.K.P. and M.C.S.

Whatever is causing the melting and thawing now wracking the Arctic, these modifications have initiated a cascade of planetwide responses that will continue even if the climate were suddenly and unexpectedly to stop warming. Imagine the climate as a big, round rock perched on uneven terrain. The inventory tells us that the rock has been pushed a little—either by a natural climate cycle or by human activity—and has started to roll. Even if the pushing stops, the rock is going to keep rolling. When it finally does stop, it will be in a completely different place than before.

To cope with the constellation of changes in the Arctic in a concerted fashion and to develop an ability to predict what will happen next rather than just react to it, several federal agencies have begun to coordinate their Arctic research in a program called SEARCH (Study of Environmental Arctic Change). Early results give some promise for success in teasing out the linkages among the tightly coupled systems that shape the climate of the Arctic and thus the earth. A recent discovery about the patterns of wind circulation, for example, helps to explain previously puzzling spatial patterns of increasing temperature [see "Winds of Change" box]. Equally important, high-quality records of climate change now extend back 30 to 50 years.

Soon these records and other findings should allow us to determine whether the Arctic transformation is a natural trend linked to emergence from the Little Ice Age or something more ominous. Our most difficult challenge in getting to that point is to come to grips with how the various feedbacks in the Arctic system interact—and to do so quickly.

More to Explore

Year on Ice Gives Climate Insights. D. K. Perovich et al. in *EOS, Transactions of the American Geophysical Union*, Vol. 80, No. 481, pages 485–486; 1999.

Global Warming and Terrestrial Ecosystems: A Conceptual Framework for Analysis. G. R. Shaver et al. in *BioScience*, Vol. 50, No. 10; 2000.

Observational Evidence of Recent Change in the Northern High-Latitude Environment. Mark Serreze et al. in *Climatic Change*, Vol. 46, pages 159–207; 2000.

The Surface Heat Budget of the Arctic Ocean (SHEBA). Special section in *Journal of Geophysical Research*, Vol. 107, No. 15; October 2002.

SEARCH Web site: http://psc.apl.washington.edu/search.

NOAA Arctic Climate Change Web site: www.ngdc.noaa.gov/paleo/sciencepub/front.htm.

About the Authors

MATTHEW STURM, DONALD K. PEROVICH and *MARK C. SERREZE* have spent most of their research careers trying to understand the snow, ice and climate of the Arctic. In 16 years at the U.S. Army Cold Regions Research and Engineering Laboratory–Alaska,

Sturm has led more than a dozen winter expeditions in Arctic Alaska, including most recently a 750-mile snowmobile traverse across the region. Perovich is with the New Hampshire office of the U.S. Army Cold Regions Research and Engineering Laboratory. His work has focused on sea ice and the ice-albedo feedback. Perovich was chief scientist on Ice Station SHEBA, a yearlong drift of an icebreaker frozen into the Arctic pack ice. Since 1986 Serreze has been with the National Snow and Ice Data Center at the University of Colorado at Boulder. His studies have emphasized Arctic climate change and interactions between sea ice and the atmosphere.

Web Sites

Due to the changing nature of Internet links, Rosen Publishing has developed an online list of Web sites related to the subject of this book. This site is updated regularly. Please use this link to access the list:

http://www.rosenlinks.com/saces/enea

For Further Reading

Barnes, Simon. *Planet Zoo: One Hundred Animals We Can't Afford to Lose*. London, England: Orion Books, Ltd, 2001.

Cohen, Daniel. *Cloning*. Revised and updated ed. Brookfield, CT: Twenty-First Century Books, 2002.

De Rothschild, David. *The Live Earth Global Warming Survival Handbook: 77 Essential Skills to Stop Climate Change—or Live Through It*. New York, NY: Rodale Books, 2007.

Dudley, William, ed. *Biodiversity* (Current Controversies). Farmington Hills, MI: Greenhaven Press, 2001.

Gore, Al. *An Inconvenient Truth: The Crisis of Global Warming*. New York, NY: Viking Books, 2007.

Ochoa, George, Jennifer Hoffman, PhD, and Tina Tin, PhD. *Climate: The Force that Shapes Our World and the Future of Life on Earth*. New York, NY: Rodale Books, 2005.

Roleff, Tamara L. *Cloning* (Opposing Viewpoints). Farmington Hills, MI: Greenhaven Press, 2005.

Schneiderman, Jill S., ed. *The Earth Around Us: Maintaining a Livable Planet*. Boulder, CO: Westview Press, 2003.

Speth, James Gustave. *Red Sky at Morning: America and the Crisis of the Global Environment*. 2nd ed. New Haven, CT: Yale University Press, 2005.

Tanaka, Shelley. *Confronting Climate Change* (World Issues Today). New York, NY: Rosen Publishing, 2008.

Viegas, Jennifer, ed. *Critical Perspectives on Planet Earth* (*Scientific American* Critical Anthologies on Environment and Climate). New York, NY: Rosen Publishing, 2007.

Wheeler, Benjamin, M.A., Gilda Wheeler, M.Ed, and Wendy Church, PhD. *It's All Connected: A Comprehensive Guide to Global Issues and Sustainable Solutions*. Seattle, WA: Facing the Future: People and the Planet, 2005.

Woodward, John, and Jennifer Skancke, eds. *Conserving the Environment* (Current Controversies). Farmington Hills, MI: Greenhaven Press, 2006.

Index